D1096167

VRS GRAF

By Emil Major and Erwin Gradmann
With a Prefatory Note by
Sir Kenneth Clark

Home & Van Thal
London

FIRST PUBLISHED 1942
BY HOLBEIN PUBLISHING COMPANY LIMITED, BASLE
FIRST PUBLISHED IN ENGLAND 1947

DESIGNED BY JAN TSCHICHOLD
PRINTED IN SWITZERLAND

The art of the Germanic countries during the period of the Reformation was the most brutal and lustful which the world has ever seen. In 1933 I happened to be engaged in the classification of sixteenth-century German woodcuts, and although usually suspicious of that too convenient abstraction, the national characteristic, I could not but be struck by the similarity of the world they revealed to that which was taking shape in Germany under the influence of the Nazis. Here in the cuts and drawings of Hans Sebald Beham, Barthel Beham, Cranach, Nicholas Manuel, and, above all, Urs Graf, was all the cruelty, the swagger, the smut, the self-pity and the hysterical virility which the political genius of Hitler and his associates had found lying dormant in a defeated people, waiting to be fanned into a final conflagration. I must apologise to my Swiss friends for classing Urs Graf as a German, but the facts of history do not always respect subsequent national sympathies. The Swiss were not always the amiable peaceful people which they have become, and the way in which the respectable merchants of Basle have survived her brutal mercenaries is a rare instance of biology and morality in combination.

Urs Graf may certainly be quoted in refutation of a narrowly moralistic theory of art. He was a cutthroat, a swindler, a bully and a lecher. He beat his wife and amused himself by abominable practical jokes. Such defects must prevent a man from being a great artist, in the sense that Dante and Michelangelo are great, but they do not prevent him from being a very good and effective one. It was Ruskin (of all unexpected people) who wrote "A good, stout, self-commanding animality is the make for poets and artists".

This animal quality of shameless self-abandonment is Urs Graf's most endearing characteristic. His superb, irresistible vitality, communicated in every flourishing line, makes all criticism of his personality seem pedantic. At times it reaches a pitch of barbarous frenzy (Plates 54 and 55) when we feel that the limits of Dionysiac art have been overstepped. But it has the effect of giving rhythmic life to a technique of drawing which, if it were not charged from some powerful dynamo, would be harsh and dry. When his animal spirits flag, Urs Graf's drawings add nothing to the late Gothic goldsmith-woodcut style common to all craftsmen of the Rhineland. True, his buccaneering expeditions to Italy brought him the knowledge of a more evolved technique, and this is sometimes reflected in his drawings—unsuccessfully in the Titianesque horse and rider in Plate 16, which may be a reminiscence of Leonardo's Sforza monument before it was destroyed by the Gascon archers; and more profitably in Plate 18 where the Venetian style is used with greater freedom. But in general he is the most uncompromisingly Northern of artists, drawing all the elements of his designs from the slashed doublets, plumes, *quillons*, codpieces, and other grotesque paraphernalia of contemporary Germanic costume. These are combined in a swirling, swaggering late Gothic style, that last echo of what Worringer called the ceaseless melody of Northern line. Throughout German art it is this rhythmic exuberance which compensates for all its crudeness and hysteria. Although a less civilised characteristic than the restraint, proportion and order of the Mediterranean, it springs directly from impulses which are at the root of artistic expression; and in consequence a Northern artist of moderate stature, like Urs Graf, is more life enhancing than his equivalent—shall we say Ridolfo Ghirlandajo or Perino del Vaga—in renaissance Italy.

But it is impossible to look at Urs Graf's drawings from a detached, æsthetic standpoint. His personality is too strong and too close to our recent experience. *Al mein gelt verspilt* says the old campaigner, probably Urs Graf himself, in the splendid drawing, Plate 14; and he seems to take a kind of perverse satisfaction in this fatality. But he had spilt much blood, too, in his effort to prove his manliness. His last work is the woodcut (Frontispiece) of a ferocious *landsknecht*, wildly plumed, who bears in his hand a banner with the date 1527. It is the year of the sack of Rome; the year in which these swaggering brutes, during weeks of torture and arson, destroyed the world of Raphael's School of Athens. Urs Graf may even have been there, for in that year he disappeared from Basle and was heard of no more.   *Kenneth Clark*

Introduction

"Pox take thee, thou snivelling lansquenet!" This heartfelt curse is a Swiss campaigner's fare-well to the wretch who refused to pledge him in a bumper, and whom he has just thrown into the tavern yard to mend his manners. The feat is hailed with a roar of appreciation by the on-lookers, soldiers of fortune like the Switzer, who lately flung their mighty two-handed swords into the corner with a resounding clang, and now sit swaggering astride the benches in their fine slashed doublets, their plumed barrets jauntily askew. Stolid artisans look on as they enjoy their evening drink and gaudy tavern wenches bestow their roving glances on the warriors. This is Basle in the year of grace 1515.

A wild, full-blooded era this, when many a man's unbounded zest for life drives him from the work-bench or the anvil and beyond the cramping confines of his native land to fight all comers and earn fine gold in Lombardy. Today he'll fight for the King of France, tomorrow for the Pope, for the Duke of Milan next, and soon for the Pope again. It is a lawless age, when men drink deep and taste life to the very dregs, savour their conquests in the arms of fiery-eyed Italian women, and yet think often of their native land. Then they picture old comrades waiting for wild tales from foreign parts and regaling themselves the while with good Swiss and Alsa-tian wines poured in a sparkling arc from high-held piggins. Now at last they are home again and, legs stretched out beneath the long narrow tables, feet firmly planted in their broad "bear-paws", they tell their tales, drink and make merry while the piper plays the old tunes; and when the thin wheezing pipes suddenly break into the ballad "O, let me always be thy love", all their mighty voices troll out the chorus.

In those days the little town, known far and wide as "merry Basle", seemed to throb with intoxicating love of life. The Union with the Confederation of 1501 had brought with it a new sense of security from foreign attack. Since then traffic had gone on its way unhindered; com-merce and industry had yielded a golden harvest. It had become easy to live and let live. Art flourished; money burnt many a pocket and flowed like quicksilver. In vain did plague and pestilence stalk the streets; the Devil took the hindermost, and life tasted all the sweeter to the living. In vain did preachers thunder against the immorality the wars had bred, against the riotous living of the men, the love of luxury and the extravagant dress of the women. It was the fashion to laugh at sermons, and to drink and whore the more. The World and the Flesh reigned supreme—and the Devil no doubt was well content.

Wherever the dance was maddest, wherever a frolic turned into a riot, there Urs Graf the goldsmith was certain to be found. No age but this of riot and sensuality could have given birth to such a man; a foul-mouthed ruffian without peer, respecting neither God nor man, ready for any piece of knavery, involved in every brawl, an adulterer and whoremonger—and an artist in every nerve. A man who, having amply proved his greatness in his own branch of art, eagerly explored fresh fields, and there too proved himself a master.

Urs was born at Soleure about 1485; his father was the goldsmith Hug Graf. His apprenticeship, probably started in his father's workshop, was completed in Basle at the turn of the century. In 1503, Graf went to Strasbourg as a travelling craftsman, and it was there that he designed his first woodcuts, twenty-five large illustrations to Ringmann's "Passion". The prints were so clumsy that the printer Schott refused them. But Urs was not in the least discouraged. He took them to his countryman, Johann Knobloch of Zofingen, who had been a burgher of Strasbourg since 1501, and plagued him until at last, in 1506, he was persuaded to publish the "Passion" series. Graf was next drawn to Zurich, where he worked as apprentice to the goldsmith Lienhart Triblin and designed woodcuts for an almanac.

1509 saw him back again in Basle, and this time it was to stay, and to marry Sibylla, daughter of the tanner Hans von Brunn in November, 1511. Although the penniless wandering apprentice had married into one of the chief burgher families of Basle, it was against the will of his father-in-law and of Sibylla's rich and childless uncle, the Junker Morand von Brunn, who disinherited her forthwith.

Graf was received into the Guild on January 19th and granted burghership on July 12th, 1512. He set up his workshop at the sign of the "Golden Rose", near the Fishmarket (now No. 18, *Stadthausgasse*) in a house which he bought in 1520[1]. The goldsmith was not long in making a name for himself. His original designs could not pass unnoticed at a time when late Gothic was still the accepted style. His cups and goblets were strangely wrought, enriched with curious arabesques; on the sheaths of his daggers, naked boys climbed amid foliage, or a woman —no slim dryad, but a buxom lass taken from life—stood naked upon a foliated scroll. Among his most popular creations were the silver barret-brooches with cheeky little boys which were soon sported by men and women alike. His wares were both witty and pretty; and above all they were up-to-date. They smacked of Italy and of what connoisseurs called the "antique" style.

And indeed Graf must have had plenty of opportunity to study Italian work at first hand. Whenever he heard the drums of war, his heart beat faster and he knew that he must follow them. On with sword and buckler, and forth into the world he strode—no matter whither, so long as there was fighting to be had. He went as far as Rome with a troop from Soleure in 1511, joined in the Basle expedition to Dijon in 1513, fought the French and the German lansquenets on the bloody field of Marignano in 1515, marched against Milan in 1521, and fought again at Bicocca the following year.

And each time he returned home laden with spoil. Ideas, drawings and sketches were the booty he brought. The goldsmith was ousted by the draughtsman. The very hand that had brandished the sword with such fiendish joy, now portrayed the turmoil and the horror of battle with terrible exactitude: the gaping head-wounds, the scattered entrails of the slain, the contorted faces of the wounded, the huge shapes of agonized horses. Camp life too provided Urs

(1) Some time ago, the present owner of the house set up a marble plaque bearing the dagger-monogram, the artist's name, and the date 1520.

with endless subjects for unrivalled figure-drawings; he noted the flaunting stride of the standard-bearers, the dignified groups of officers in conclave, the bands of wastrels and feckless *vivandières*, and the men-at-arms of every type and clime. His travels revealed to him the pictorial qualities of landscape. He was among the first to draw pure landscape: lake and mountain scenes, with castle, tower and bridge, or sometimes a little township amid the plain.

But it was in recording the everyday sights of Basle that he chiefly excelled. Whether they are noted in a few cogent lines, or worked out in elaborate detail, such drawings reveal an unrivalled virtuosity. Who had ever shown such skill in depicting a recruiting scene in the Guild Chamber? Who had ever dared to make fun of a respectable married couple from behind?— or to draw a wanton beauty so that her wantonness was branded on her face?

These malicious drawings delighted his contemporaries and the master printers of Basle, among them Johann Amerbach, Adam Petri, and Johannes Froben, were quick to exploit their popularity. From 1509 onwards, Urs was overwhelmed with orders for woodcuts; for a time scarcely a book appeared in Basle without his collaboration. His woodcuts for the Basle and Strasbourg printers are to be reckoned by the hundred. Here too he was the pioneer of a new style, already clearly formulated in his Basle illustrations of 1511. Always on the lookout for something new, he sometimes experimented with white-on-black woodcuts, which were partly engraved so as to produce white lines upon the black figure. In this technique he produced the spirited "Sixteen Standard-bearers of the Confederate States" published in 1521.

Even then he was not satisfied, but turned to engraving on copper, an art for which his skill as a silver chaser well fitted him. By 1513 he had also fully mastered the art of etching. He had apprenticed himself in 1511 to the glass-painter Hans Heinrich Wolleb of Basle, had designed heraldic glass-paintings, and had even painted on glass himself, conforming to the latest taste by working in grisaille. From glass-painting to painting on wood was a short step. Graf painted a panel, a "St. George and the Dragon", as sturdy and secular a saint as ever slew monster.

Then, one fine morning Basle rang with Graf's latest success, a broadsheet ballad of his own composing. The verses, intended only to be sung, have outlived the work of many a contemporary poet and show how completely Graf was in tune with popular tradition. Underlying their delicious spontaneity is a certain Gothic grace, a troubadour-eloquence suggestive of an earlier origin. Even the decorative borders of the broadsheet were not original: Graf evidently took them from old blocks, and parts of them are very like the borders of Johann Amerbach's *Zitglögglyn*, published in 1492.

Thus sang Graf in his youth[1]. His disillusioned mood at thirty-three produced the bitter, laconic rhyme: *Ursüs Graff Daz tültig schaff*—Urs Graf, tame as a sheep (Plate 100). But the "bear" was still anything but tamed. He was more to be believed at twenty-seven when he signed a drawing *Düfelskopf*—Devil's head—(Plate 50).

He was an unfailing source of scandal. Time and again he was brought to court to answer for his unruly tongue. He was imprisoned in 1511 for mocking a priest, sentenced in 1513 for using obscene abuse to a tailor, and fined in 1514 for calling the coachmaker Claus Fesser a

(1) See illustration p. 11.

lansquenet. So bitter was the enmity between Swiss and German mercenaries, that the epithet "lansquenet" had become a punishable insult in the Swiss law courts. After the battle of Marignano in 1515, the legend was current in Switzerland that the Germans killed on that field had refused to await the Judgment side by side with the Swiss, but unfurling a white flag with a red cross upon it had marched as one man to the Gates of Heaven.

Graf's boon companion was the goldsmith Hans Öder. They had fought side by side at Marignano and were rogues of the same breed. In June 1522 they were both imprisoned in the Tower in Basle because they "took service in the war and therein did defy their authorities' ordinance". Graf was imprisoned again in the summer of the next year, this time for inciting to sedition by saying repeatedly in a tavern "Ough! How cold it is here!", in transparent allusion to the warmth of Italy, land of forbidden wars. But here in the dungeon, on August 12th, 1523, he was to know the greatest triumph of his life. A great shooting contest was to be held in Basle. The competitors from every part of the Confederation had already assembled. They were quick to note the absence of one of the keenest marksmen of all, their former comrade and boon companion, Urs Graf. They could not do without Graf; somehow he would have to be there. So a deputation waited upon the Council, who agreed that the occasion warranted clemency, and set their prisoner free.

Graf's nocturnal exploits were less to his credit. On more than one occasion he was committed to the *Spalenturm* for midnight pranks worthy of Pantagruel. His name became notorious, and the coarser his latest practical joke, the louder was the obscene delight of all but the victim. One night in April 1523, Christian Guldinpek the stonemason and a companion were walking up the narrow *Riesengässlein* near the Fishmarket, past Hans Öder's house, when certain pots were emptied upon their heads from an upper window. In reply to their volley of curses and threats, Hans only threw the pots after. Then Urs Graf joined in. He and Öder pursued their victims to the Fishmarket and there fell on them with drawn swords. Another trick played by Graf and some students, this time upon the night watch, the police constabulary of the period, was immortalised in a collection of notable knaveries[1]. The story runs:

There was once a goldsmith of Basle, a free master, named Urs Graf. He induced two students of the town to help him in a trick; at dead of night they were to stretch a rope across the street from his house and then to make enough clamour to bring all the watch running—the prettiest piece of ropery ever plotted! They came that very night and Graf showed them how to loop the rope round the grating of the cellar opposite and bring it back, so that both ends hung down in his own cellar. All was ready to begin when they espied one of the watchmen humped up against the wall of a house, fast asleep, his morion by his side. The pair carried off the helmet, filled it with filth from the street gutter and nimbly replaced it. Then they crept up towards the *Eisengasse*, drew their sabres and clashed them lustily together. The clamour drew the watch from every side. The briskest tripped first: here fell a halberd, there rolled the man, away bowled his helmet; there two or three lashed about them in a heap. The slumberer, awaking suddenly, and making to clap his helmet on and run to the scene of action, forthwith anointed himself with the stinking filth, "and there he sat all bemoiled and bemused, a sight most piteous!" Meanwhile, Graf sat in his cellar and looked to the rope. When the watch began to sort themselves out,

(1) Jacob Frey, "Die Garten Geselschaft", 1556, Ch. 90.

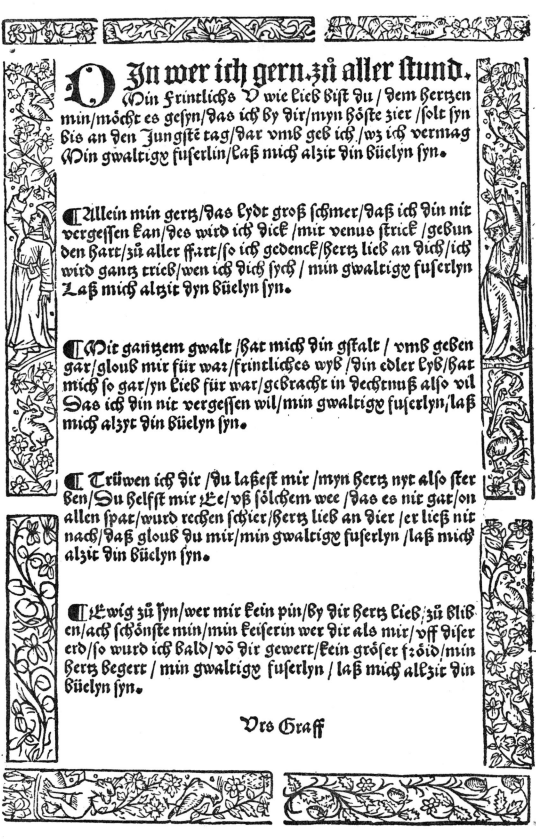

O In wer ich gern, zů aller stund.
Min frintlichs O wie lieb bist du / dem hertzen
min / möcht es gesyn / das ich by dir / myn höste zier / solt syn
bis an den Jungstē tag / dar vmb geb ich / wz ich vermag
Min gwaltigy fuserlin / laß mich alzit din büelyn syn.

Allein min gertz / das lydt groß schmer / daß ich din nit
vergessen kan / des wird ich dick / mit venus strick / gebun
den hart / zů aller ffirt / so ich gedenck / hertz lieb an dich / ich
wird gantz trieb / wen ich dich sych / min gwaltigy fuserlyn
Laß mich alzit dyn büelyn syn.

Mit gantzem gwalt / hat mich din gstalt / vmb geben
gar / gloub mir für war / frintliches wyb / din edler lyb / hat
mich so gar / yn lieb für war / gebracht in dechtnuß also vil
Das ich din nit vergessen wil / min gwaltigy fuserlyn / laß
mich alzyt din büelyn syn.

Trüwen ich dir / du laßest mir / myn hertz nyt also ster
ben / Du helfst mir Ee / vß sölchem wee / das es nit gar / on
allen spar / wurd rechen schier / hertz lieb an dier / er ließ nit
nach / daß gloub du mir / min gwaltigy fuserlyn / laß mich
alzit din büelyn syn.

Ewig zů syn / wer mir kein pin / by dir hertz lieb, zů bliß
en / ach schönste min / min keiserin wer dir als mir / vff diser
erd / so wurd ich bald / võ dir gewert / kein gröser fröid / min
hertz begert / min gwaltigy fuserlyn / laß mich alzit din
büelyn syn.

Vrs Graff

fumbling for their weapons in the dark, he let go one end of the rope and ripped the other quickly back into the cellar. Then he went up into the dark house, lit a lantern, and ran out into the street to discover what all the noise was about. Grumbling and cursing at this disturbance of his rest, he lighted the watch while they found their weapons, and joined them in their search for the night birds ...

Graf committed a more serious offence one night in 1518, when he attacked and crippled a total stranger "without a word". To elude the law, he fled to Soleure, where he remained in exile for a year. Soon after this "murderous business", on August 13th, 1518, the Council order- ed an inventory of the contents of Graf's house. The document testifies to the unpretentious comfort in which he lived. A bath gown is conspicuous among his linen; he had taken with him his best clothes, his sword and his dagger, leaving only a black skull-cap and four worn-out pairs of hose. Besides such personal effects, he had left his cross-bow, halberd and old jousting arms, his goldsmith's tools, and two silver-mounted utensils. A wooden panel with a chalk ground, a small painted panel and three boxes of colour showed that he was a painter. The ground floor of his house was given up to his shop and workshop. On the first floor, facing the street, was the living-room, furnished with table, chairs, ewers and other chattels, and behind it was a well-equipped kitchen. On the second floor was the bedroom with double-bed, a cot for young Graf, born towards the end of 1512, and a few chests. At the back was a guest-chamber. The apprentice slept in the attic.

Such were the surroundings in which Sibylla von Brunn lived with Urs whenever he chanced not to be exiled, imprisoned or at the wars. We meet her comely rounded face in many of Graf's drawings (Plates 19, 20, 68 and 79). It is the face of a gentle kind-hearted woman. How different was Graf himself! Legal documents reveal him as a lawless devil, headstrong, passion- ate, malicious and vengeful. His self-portraits (Plates 14, 18, 26, 32) reflect no more flattering image. He was broadly and powerfully built; his war-like hooked nose, deeply cleft at the root, his long heavy jowl and jutting chin lend an air of permanence to his malevolent expression. As a young man he was clean-shaven[1] and only later took to the pointed beard and long moustache with its barbarically drooping ends. There exists another portrait of him. In 1522 Hans Holbein the Younger painted a Madonna commissioned by the Basle Chancellor Hans Gerster for presentation to Soleure Cathedral. To St. Ursus, who stands on the right of the Virgin, Holbein gave Graf's features. The saint's moustache is reddish-brown, and a Basle court record confirms this indication that Urs was red-haired. Graf was prosecuting Claus Harnasch for having gravely insulted him by calling him "Urs Goldsmith thou damned red rogue!"

With such a husband Sibylla can have known little of connubial bliss, and legal documents suggest that at times her life was well-nigh unbearable. Graf was not an attentive husband; he treated her worse than a slave, beat her, and spent his time with loose women. On November 20th, 1522, he was released from the *Wasserturm*, where he had been imprisoned for "living lustfully, consorting openly and impudently with jades and harlots, walking in adultery, and treating

(1) Cf. Plate 26. Some time ago (in 1907) I suggested 1512 as the date of this drawing; I now accept Koegler's dating ca. 1508 as the more probable. At the same time, I still hold that it represents Graf in his youth. If we accept this date, the woman on the right can of course no longer be identified as Sibylla, whom he married in 1511.

basely and uncouthly his own lawful wife with knocks and blows". He was made to swear that in future he would not "strike, beat, pinch, squeeze, or otherwise offend" her, but would "treat her as beseemeth an honest wife, and behave himself worthily as a good husband". He was publicly warned that he should in future "beware of falling into such a scandalous life of adultery and other wilfulness".

Despite these misdemeanours, Graf the artist was an indispensable and highly esteemed member of the community. His woodcuts, both monotypes and book decorations, found purchasers and imitators not only in Basle and in his native town of Soleure, but in all the outlying provinces. The proofs he took of his chased-silver work were used abroad as patterns (Cf. description of Plates 101–104). When Erhard Kastler, Abbot of St. Urban's Monastery in the Canton of Lucerne, decided to present a large silver bust of St. Bernard to his monastery, he ordered it from Urs Graf, then an exile in Soleure (Plate 116). Graf received his pardon towards the end of 1519, and returned to Basle to be at once appointed die-cutter to the Mint by a far-sighted Council. In this capacity, he designed new dies and, with his delightful image of the Virgin, first introduced the half-length human figure into the Basle coinage. It was not without a certain pride that he signed a page written in 1523 in his own secret cipher (Plate 126), the obverse of which (Plate 18) bears a self-portrait, "By me, Ursus Graf, goldsmith and die-cutter to the mint in Basle".

This page is interesting for another reason; it affords unequivocal proof that Graf was in touch with Lutheran circles. The enciphered text is a German version of the ancient antiphon to the Holy Ghost still used in the Roman Catholic liturgy: *Veni sancte spiritus, reple tuorum corda fidelium* .... It is well known that Luther and his followers translated certain Latin hymns and used them in German services. Many of these hymns were first printed in single sheets, and the earliest we know are dated 1523. The *Enchiridion*, published in Erfurt under Luther's supervision in 1524, was the first German hymn book and is based on these earlier hymn sheets. The hymn to the Holy Ghost which it contains differs considerably from Graf's translated text (1), whereas the version in the second Erfurt *Enchiridion* of 1527 closely resembles Graf's (2).

It seems highly probable that Graf had seen one of these German hymn sheets. The hymn must have impressed him since he copied it out. As a faithful son of the Catholic Church, anxious to avoid falling under false suspicion of heresy, he was careful to write it in cipher. Perhaps he was also a little ashamed of this sudden fit of piety. In any case, the document gives us our first inkling of Graf's inner life. It is evidence of the dualism in his character. His work reveals on the one hand a native coarseness and brutality intensified by camp life, on the other an acute artistic sensibility and an appreciation of religious values. Such a dualism would account for the strange contrast between the caricature of St. George and the Dragon (Plate 55) and the moving "Man of Sorrows" of 1525 (Plate 59), between the comfortable bourgeoise Virgin (Plate 100) and the gracious Queen of Heaven (Plate 111).

In his later years Graf's wildness seems to have abated. We hear of only one more appearance

(1) Fr. Zelle, Das älteste lutherische Haus-Gesangbuch 1524, Göttingen 1903, pp. 2, 3, 114/115.
(2) Joh. Zahn, Die Melodien der deutschen evangelischen Kirchenlieder, Vol. 5, Gütersloh 1892, p. 265.

in court, and this time as a witness. We can assign no drawing from his hand to the years 1526 and 1527. His last work was the beautiful white-on-black woodcut, "The Standard-bearer" (Frontispiece), the blocks of which he himself elaborated with the burin in 1527. He probably died in the same year, certainly not later than the spring of 1528, but where and in what manner we do not know. He was in his forty-fourth year.

Sibylla did not mourn him overlong. On October 13th, 1528, she married the cutler Thoman Wels of Basle. Graf had left her a twofold legacy. First there was his son Urs, who became a goldsmith like his father, but was not of much account. He moved to Soleure in 1553 and died in the Romagna in 1560. Of incomparably greater worth and importance were the artistic remains which Sibylla inherited, and of which the greater part later became the property of the *Amerbach-Kabinett* in Basle. Designs for goldsmith's work, engravings on silver and copper, designs for glass-painting, and a large number of drawings now form part of the Basle Museum: some drawings and engravings have passed into foreign collections.

Today it is with astonishment and admiration that we realise the variety of Graf's artistic output. His goldsmith's work alone easily surpassed most contemporary production, but the spontaneous creations of the free artist, the drawings and engravings, reveal the sure and life-giving touch of the master, the independence and ruthless honesty of the genius. These are the works that make Graf's name immortal.

Emil Major

Notes on the Reproductions

The dimensions given for drawings are those of the paper; engravings are measured from edge to edge of the print. Height precedes width. The full titles of the books cited will be found in the bibliographical index (Page 38).

Frontispiece

Standard-bearer

White-on-black woodcut. 8 × 4 7/8 in. Dated 1527. Unsigned. Original block in Basle: Öffentliche Kunstsammlung. [His 300; K. 179]

Even Graf's most accomplished work confirms the impression that he never completely freed himself from the artistic conventions of the Middle Ages: his art remained based on the formal conceptions and guided by the precepts of the craftsman's workshop. Occasionally he defied them and produced drawings remarkable for their expressive power, but too often relapsed again into conventional mediocrity. This conflict may well be the source of some of his satirical drawings which are deliberate parodies of convention. Graf's genius cannot be called universal: it revealed itself only in the portrayal of single figures. In that field he achieved his masterpieces. His reiteration of typical pose and gesture may appear to be merely a formal device, but it demands to be judged for its effectiveness. It is from this point of view that we can best appreciate his last known work, in which Graf succeeded in giving an astonishing effect of impetus to his marching figure. The print is particularly interesting for another reason: in contrast with Graf's other white-on-black woodcuts (Cf. Plates 123–125), in which the technique of the woodcarver is unmistakable, this print shows a pure engraving technique to which the exceptionally fine inner lines of the figure are due. We may assume that Graf, not content with drawing the figure on the block, himself engraved the lines which were to appear in white against the black ground.

I

Half-length Figure of a richly dressed young Woman

Pen drawing. 10 × 8 1/4 in. Dated 1518. Signed: VG monogram above a Swiss dagger. Basle: Öffentliche Kunstsammlung. [K.81]

In spite of the elaborate detail in which her elegant dress is drawn, Graf has lost nothing of this young woman's fundamental sensuality. The curves of her body are noted as deliberately as the structure of her finery. We are made aware that her bent head and coy expression, and the sinuous pose of her arm – like the paw of a playful cat – are consciously arranged to court admiring glances. Her lofty brow was artificially obtained by shaving the hair away from her forehead, in accordance with a fashion peculiar to the Renaissance. Graf did not overlook this additional charm. A waving pheasant's feather is fastened to her cap by a silver medallion, the fashionable barret-brooch: a cross of St. Antony hangs on her breast as an amulet against the pla-

gue, and a heavy chain of precious metal encircles her shoulders. The sleeve of this vain beauty is heavily adorned with four apes' heads and a thick tuft of bristles, the hair brush of the period. On the under edge of her barret is a winged M surmounted by a coronet (Cf. Plate 31).

2

Half-length Figure of a young Man with a Pocket-sundial

Pen drawing. 7 1/2 × 5 7/8 in. Circa 1508 (Parker). Signed: separated initials V G and borax box. Basle: Robert von Hirsch Collection.

The young man in a fur-lined houppelande, his head slightly bent, eyes half-closed against the dazzling sunlight, is intent on setting his watch in accordance with the sun's position. The timepiece, which he has taken out of its brass case, is a *Concavum* (scil. horologium). The silver agraffe decorating his barret has the unusual form of an opening pea-pod. Barret-pins of this kind, embellished with human or animal figures, flowers, fruit, initials or even all sorts of familiar household objects, were part of fashionable dress in Graf's day.

This is one of Graf's finest portrait-drawings, admirable not only for the delicate observation it reveals and its masterly formal construction but also for its rendering of material quality with the simplest means. It is uncertain whether Graf based this work, like so many others, on some picture known to him. In any case his interest in the treatment of such a subject proves the wide artistic capacity latent in the young draughtsman. Although the composition echoes the pictorial concepts of the late Gothic period, the figure has clarity and depth.

Both the style of the monogram and the addition of the borax box characterise this drawing as an early work.

3

Half-length Figure of a smiling Woman

Pen drawing. 10 5/8 × 7 7/8 in. Dated 1525. Signed: Dagger monogram. Dessau: Anhaltische Behördenbibliothek. [P. 15]

It is interesting to compare this drawing with the portrait of a young woman drawn seven years earlier (Cf. Plate 1). The later work shows no essential progress in composition: even the contour of shoulder and bosom is scarcely changed. On the other hand, the figure is now more closely adapted to the frame, while the covetous sidelong glance leaves us in no doubt as to the woman's nature.

The obviously lively interest with which Graf studied this type of woman did not stop short at her fashionable dress, every detail of which is lovingly portrayed. Its most striking features are the wide barret which surmounts the coif and has a medallion of a Triton pinned under its brim, and the damask tippet, turned back at the throat to reveal the pearl-mounted pendant with the crowned initials MV.

4

Head and Shoulders of a bearded King

Pen drawing. $6^{1}/_{2} \times 5^{1}/_{8}$ in. 1510 (Parker). Signed: VG monogram and borax box. Paris: Ecole des Beaux-Arts. [P. 24]

When Graf drew this head, he was still a young man, who executed diligently and perseveringly every commission that came his way, and often copied without considering his personal bent. His artistic personality was still latent, only to emerge the more distinctly in his mature work. Graf may well have "composed" this drawing from the pages of a book of Gothic designs. The man's stern features and the luxurious beard of corkscrew curls which cannot hide the clumsy contour of his shoulders both suggest such an origin, while the writing whorls on his hat and the spread-eagle were details familiar to every goldsmith.

The diadem with crocket-like prongs that surrounds the hat shows that we are in the presence of a king—probably one of the Magi, who wear this same headgear in many Gothic pictures of the Adoration (Major).

5

Soldier on the Shore of a Lake

Pen drawing. $8^{1}/_{2} \times 6^{1}/_{4}$ in. Dated 1514. Signed: VG monogram. Basle: Öffentliche Kunstsammlung. [K. 47]

In the foreground of a rapidly sketched landscape, stands the mighty figure of a bareheaded veteran with his back towards us. In this variant of Graf's favourite theme, the relation of the figure to the background is particularly happy. The warrior's right hand rests on the shaft of his pike: his left grasps the hilt of his sword. His Swiss dagger is stuck crosswise into the back of his belt, ready to be drawn with the right hand.

6

The Vine Grower

Pen sketch. $9^{3}/_{8} \times 7^{1}/_{8}$ in. Probably 1513 (Koegler), 1514 (Major). Signed: VG monogram. Basle: Öffentliche Kunstsammlung. [K. 20]

The emaciated, stubble-bearded vine-tender stands in a servile attitude, his right hand clutching his hat with its three scanty cock's feathers, while with the other hand he supports a sack slung over his left shoulder. A pruning knife is stuck into his belt at the back, while at his right side dangles a long dirk. The livery band on his right sleeve proclaims him (according to Major) to be a serf of the Cistercian Monastery of St. Urban in the Canton of Lucerne (Cf. Plate 116).

Documents testify that Urs was commissioned in the spring of 1514 to repair a monstrance for the monastery. It was prob-

ably at that time that he made this sketch, the quality of which is evidence of Graf's increasing interest in the study from life and its expressionistic potentialities.

7

A Soldier

Pen drawing. $8^{1}/_{2} \times 6^{1}/_{4}$ in. Dated 1514. Signed: VG monogram. Basle: Öffentliche Kunstsammlung. [K. 46]

Even if we did not know Graf to have been a seasoned campaigner, this drawing alone would afford convincing proof that his soldiers are not merely the creatures of a lively imagination, but were born of the artist's own experience. Such a picture could have been drawn only at first hand, by one to whom such figures were part and parcel of daily life, comrades in rape, murder, pillage and arson. The whole history of soldiering is summed up in the truculent strength of this mercenary, who bestrides his ground so uncompromisingly. Slashed clothes, ragged hose, half-naked legs, three different weapons—sword, dagger and pike—and a brutal cast of countenance are the hallmarks of this ruffian.

8–9

Two Standard-bearers

Silver point drawings. $5^{1}/_{2} \times 3^{3}/_{4}$ and $5^{1}/_{4} \times 3^{3}/_{8}$ in. Circa 1520/21 (Koegler). Unsigned. Basle: Öffentliche Kunstsammlung. [K. 93, 91a]

These unsigned drawings belong to a series of ten studies which were collected together in a sketch book. All ten are various renderings of the pose and movements of a standard-bearer with sword and flagstaff. The studies, either imaginary or based on some works known to Graf, were used by him in 1521 for the series of woodcuts "The Sixteen Standard-bearers of the Confederate States". Comparison with the white-on-black woodcuts (Cf. Plates 123–124) shows that Graf did not use either of these designs without considerable alteration.

These drawings in silver point, a medium rarely used by Graf, are fine examples of his free inventive style.

10

Young Soldier holding a Pike

Pen drawing. $8^{3}/_{4} \times 6^{1}/_{4}$ in. Probably 1513 (Koegler). Signed: VG monogram. Basle: Öffentliche Kunstsammlung. [K. 19]

In the energetic gesture of the young warrior's arm, Graf hit upon an arresting symbol for the call to arms, to which his incisive penmanship gives fullest effect. The skin-tight hose of the soldier's right leg contrasts with the wildly fringed trunk-hose of the left, the lower part of which is bare. The ornament at the tip of the pike and the peculiar shape of the dagger are of interest to the student of costume.

11

Nude Youth

Pen drawing. $8^{1}/_{2} \times 5^{5}/_{8}$ in. Dated 1512. Signed: VG monogram. Basle: Öffentliche Kunstsammlung. [K. 14]

The quasi-Renaissance style and composition of this drawing are surprising in a work of Graf. The figure is outlined in bold pen strokes and the inner modelling, though summary, reveals a sure hand. Less skilful is the manner in which the artist endeavoured to detach the figure from the mass of the tree trunk: he used heavy shading, stressed uncertainties of contour, and then seems suddenly to have yielded to his temperament and hastily completed the work so painstakingly begun.

Graf was not deeply interested in the male nude, especially when, as in this drawing, it was to be represented in an unrelated, purely statuesque pose. He seems to have been influenced unconsciously by the idea of a woman's body, a subject he was well able to draw. The bent knee and outswung hip are characteristic of his female figures.

This drawing was used in the following year as model for a St. Sebastian on a barret-brooch (Cf. Plate 111).

12

A young Dandy in Battle-array

Pen drawing. $12 \frac{1}{4} \times 8$ in. Dated 1519. Signed: Dagger monogram. Basle: Öffentliche Kunstsammlung. [K. 83]

This vacant-looking youth wears the name of his beloved "MERGILI : HEILMAN : VON : B" embroidered on a riband across his chest. Graf apparently intended to satirise this silly parade by giving his love-lorn hero the expression of a moon-struck half-wit which makes a ridiculous contrast with the splendour of his richly plumed barret, modishly slashed doublet, and highly polished armour.

Merga or Mergili Heilman of Basle, daughter of the tailor Hans Heilman, was married first to the tailor Mathis Gerster, and the second time to Benedikt Knup, the Basle painter who sold his house at the sign of the "Golden Rose" to Graf in October 1520 (Major).

13

Plumed Soldier of Fortune

Pen sketch. $8 \frac{3}{8} \times 6 \frac{1}{8}$ in. Dated 1523. Signed: Dagger monogram. Basle: Öffentliche Kunstsammlung. [K. 110]

Satirical intent and sheer delight in the play of line combined to inspire this spirited parody of a soldier armed with Swiss sword, pike and ornate Swiss dagger, and determined to enhance his appearance with the greatest possible number of plumes. It is a biting satire of the exaggerated show of plumes in which some soldiers of fortune indulged (Cf. Plate 12).

14

The Return of the Mercenary

Pen drawing. A considerable part has been cut out along the contour lines. $10 \frac{3}{4} \times 7 \frac{3}{4}$ in. Dated 1519. Signed: Dagger monogram. Basle: Öffentliche Kunstsammlung. [K. 84]

In sullen rage, with long sloping strides, the soldier marches homeward, carrying on his left shoulder his mighty battle-worn two-handed sword. The inscription on the blade: "AL MEIN GELT VERSPILT 1519" (All my money spilt 1519) is illustrated by the leaking purse which hangs from it and tells the usual story of hardearned wages lost at dice. The soldier wears a leather cap with earflaps and adorned with a feather; a heavy leathern apron reaches to his knees. A raven accompanies him, croaking derisively. Aslant his body hangs a short broadsword of the type used by German lansquenets, with quillons forming a figure-eight. This was occasionally worn by the Swiss, who adopted it from their rivals in place of the longer Swiss sword. It can be recognised by its symmetrical fan-shaped hilt and horizontal figure-of-eight guard, whose curved quillons were usually tipped with balls. (E. A. Geßler, *Führer durch die Waffensammlung des Schweizerischen Landesmuseums* 1928, p. 20) This sword is worn in several of Graf's drawings by the Swiss: by a soldier in the "Flute Serenade" drawing (Plate 45), the standard-bearer in the woodcut dated 1527 (Frontispiece), and by the "Fortuna" (Plate 64). A captain from Uri wears a similar weapon in Diebold Schilling's *Luzerner Bilderchronik* of 1513 (Plate 226, Geneva edition, 1932). The two-handed sword, a weapon of Swiss origin, also appears with large figure-of-eight quillons in the form given to it by the German lansquenets (Cf. Plates 8, 12 and 151).

Major regards the eloquently drawn soldier as a self-portrait in which Urs vented his spleen upon himself.

15

Standard-bearer

Pen drawing: white ink on dark purplish-brown paper. $12 \frac{1}{8} \times 8 \frac{5}{8}$ in. Dated 1514. Signed: VG monogram. Basle: Öffentliche Kunstsammlung. [K. 45]

With long springy strides, the standard-bearer marches from right to left of the page, his right hand grasping the folds of his proudly waving colours. The white flashes on the dark background suggest the stormy atmosphere which precedes the battle.

The drawing is a masterpiece of clean line; it exercises the fascination of a simple pictorial effect perfectly achieved. Graf borrowed this particularly effective technique from contemporary German artists, notably from Hans Baldung. In his "Sixteen Standard bearers of the Confederate States", published in 1521, Graf achieved a similar effect on wood blocks, thus in his turn influencing the development of German graphic art.

16

Horseman in Armour with a Battle-hammer

Pen drawing. $6 \frac{1}{2} \times 6$ in. Circa 1519 (Koegler). Signed: Dagger monogram. Basle: Öffentliche Kunstsammlung [K. 87]

This rather crude drawing lays no claim to pictorial effect. The artist probably attempted the subject in connection with some larger work, but did not succeed in establishing any pictorial relationship between horse and rider.

Here again the form is defined by outline alone; inner drawing and shading are arbitrary and hasty. Graf was disinclined by temperament to waste much time on the study of anatomy and movement. Whatever he could not draw successfully at the outset, or perfect by making several trial versions, was finished off quickly, tricked out with a grandiloquent monogram and cast aside.

17

Standard-bearer and Camp-follower

Pen drawing. 12¹/₂ × 8¹/₂ in. Dated 1516. Signed: V G monogram. Basle: Öffentliche Kunstsammlung. [K. 70]

The Standard-bearer marches across a knoll in the foreground, carrying a flag that waves in the breeze; energy and grim determination keep his eyes fixed upon some distant goal.

His baggage-carrier follows on a lower path, bearing his master's leather knapsack and long pike, from which dangles a stolen goose. By the wayside stands a shrine roughly hewn from a tree-trunk: behind it are trees with lightly sketched foliage. The straight lines of flagstaff, sword and pike give the picture direction and movement. Errors of perspective, such as the cutting of the shrine by the pike, cannot detract from the impression of irresistibly forward-marching destiny conveyed by the whole drawing. It is on the whole a masterpiece both in design and in execution.

18

Rich Burgher reading the Inscription on a Tablet

Pen sketch. 12¹/₄ × 7¹/₈ in. 1523 (Major, Koegler). Signed: V G monogram. Basle: Öffentliche Kunstsammlung. [K. 111]

A prosperous middle-aged burgher with a houppelande thrown over his shoulders, his left hand on the pommel of his sword, his right, with a signet ring on the index finger, resting on his hip, is studying a tablet that hangs on a tree. We can guess the word "POEMA" on the tablet thanks to the pious inscription made by Graf in secret cipher on the reverse of the page (Cf. Plate 126) and dated 1523. Major regards the figure as a self-portrait.

The drawing, a mere sketch, gives a good idea of Graf's method. Contour and inner lines are all drawn at the same time; essentials only are rapidly indicated. Heavy pen strokes are added afterwards to give life and accent to the figure.

19

Mother and Child

Pen drawing. 8¹/₂ × 6¹/₄ in. Dated 1514. Signed: V G monogram. Basle: Öffentliche Kunstsammlung. [K. 30]

The fundamental joys and sorrows of life rarely find expression in Graf's work, but this drawing moves us by its direct and simple evocation of pure happiness, while leaving us in no doubt as to its authorship.

Graf could have found no better model than his young wife Sibylla as she held her wriggling baby in her arms. Her steady gaze holds a momentary question, and yet seems withdrawn in deep contentment.

20

Young Woman carrying Apples in the Fold of her Skirt

Pen drawing. 8³/₈ × 6¹/₈ in. Dated 1514. Signed: V G monogram. Basle: Öffentliche Kunstsammlung. [K. 38]

In the naïvely posed figure, we recognise Graf's wife Sibylla von Brunn. The jagged crown which adorns her graceful head is the attribute of a pagan goddess: the apples she holds in the

fulness of her skirt symbolise fruitfulness. She wears a dagger in her girdle on the left hip. On the ground lies a small pocket-sundial of wood or bone shaped like a diptych after the fashion of the time.

21

Courtesan holding a Pair of Scales

Pen drawing. 6¹/₄ × 4⁵/₈ in. Circa 1516 (Koegler). Signed: VG monogram. Basle: Öffentliche Kunstsammlung [K. 65]

This venal beauty trails forward towards the left of the picture, the scales held out in her right hand: her long gown drags on the ground and a bedraggled feather nods from the barret, worn tilted over her network coif.

Her jewelry consists of a massive shoulder-chain and a necklet of precious metal bearing the initials "KKH .. M". Her male partner is evidently Graf himself whose initials V and G are weighed in the scales. The lady advertises her profession by her uncovered breasts and boldly lifted skirt.

22

Young Woman holding a Sword of State

Pen drawing. 7³/₄ × 7¹/₈ in. Dated 1518. Signed: V G monogram. Basle: Öffentliche Kunstsammlung. [K. 79]

A generously proportioned young woman advances barefoot towards the artist's reversed monogram, which is legible from where she stands. Her left hand holds a long two-handed sword whose elaborate hilt has a cube-shaped pommel and a double-arched guard. Her gown is so lavishly looped over her raised right arm that one leg is bared to the thigh: this gesture of gallantry is underlined by the inscription on her bodice: "O ANELI ICH WOT GERN" (Oh, Annie, I should love to ...).

23

Young Woman stepping into the Water

Pen drawing. 8 × 6 in. Probably 1513 (Parker), considerably later according to Koegler. Signed: Dagger monogram and Basle staff. Vienna: Albertina. [P. 36; K. 134]

Over her richly embroidered hair-net, this elegant young woman wears a barret adorned with a pheasant's feather. The fine cambric chemisette visible above her bodice is deeply slashed and tied in front with ribbons. Graf dwelt with obvious pleasure on the full curves of her body and bare legs framed by the gracefully lifted skirt. Errors of drawing, such as the clumsy over-shortening of the right leg, are details that seem unimportant in Graf's work. The decorative curves of the figure and the quiet depth of the landscape background give to this drawing its peculiar charm.

24

Flying Putti

Pen drawing. 4 × 11¹/₂ in. Circa 1514 (Koegler, Major). Unsigned. Basle: Öffentliche Kunstsammlung. [K. 41]

Nine *putti* holding diverse objects are flying about in space, unrelated to one another except by the rollicking pattern of their inconsequent antics. As a book-illustrator, Graf was well versed in the plump jointlessness of infant anatomy and it is characteristic that he should have given free reign to his fancy in the treatment of a subject usually bound by the strict requirements of a decorative border.

25

Young Woman surrounded by Putti

Pen drawing. $6^{1}/_{4} \times 8^{3}/_{8}$ in. Dated 1514. Signed: VG monogram. Basle: Öffentliche Kunstsammlung. [K. 40]

Four *putti* armed with spears, shield and dagger, press round a young woman who stands resignedly with her hands crossed beneath her bosom; a fifth *putto* brandishes a baby's bib on a long forked stick. The meaning of the picture seems to be that, after the joys of love, Cupid flies away and the woman is beset by sorrow and pain, here represented by her little besiegers, until motherhood sets her free. Perhaps the drawing was inspired by the thought of Sibylla, whom Graf had portrayed in the same year in the sweetly acquiescent pose of a Madonna. The cupid flying away is reminiscent of Dürer's engraving "The three Genii" (B. 66).

26

A Mercenary with a Woman and two Children

Pen drawing. $7^{1}/_{4} \times 9^{1}/_{8}$ in. Circa 1508 (Koegler). Signed: VG monogram and borax box. Basle: Öffentliche Kunstsammlung. [K. 5]

The thick-set, rather clumsy figure of the soldier fills the left half of the picture. A little further back on the right stands a young woman with a baby in her arms, while a second child hides under her skirt. The pike planted in the ground (a pair of clogs tied to its shaft), divides the picture which in any case lacks unity and is devoid of any special interest unless we regard it as an autobiographical document. In fact Major believes it to be a self-portrait.

27

A young Girl

Pen drawing. $5^{1}/_{2} \times 3^{3}/_{4}$ in. Probably 1514 (Koegler). Signed: VG monogram. Basle: Öffentliche Kunstsammlung. [K. 32]

The graceful stance and unstudied gesture of the girl are sensitively drawn. But how immeasurably the composition gains by the masterly penstroke that caused the blade of grass to spring up on her left! It not only gives balance to the picture, but is in itself a manifestation of the power of line, which, like the single word, comes to life only when it is used in a special rhythmic relationship to give an image the very accent of its creator.

28

Lovers beside a Lake

Pen drawing. $6^{1}/_{8} \times 4^{1}/_{4}$ in. Circa 1512/13 (Koegler). Signed: VG monogram. Basle: Öffentliche Kunstsammlung. [K. 18]

Of all Graf's drawings of lovers, this is the most charming. Graf's customary coarse directness here gives place to a sincerely lyrical rendering of the ardent wooing. The scene is laid on the shore of a lake. On the right a little copse, on the left tall slender reeds form a frame for the lovers. The S-shaped object in the foreground has no connection with the drawing itself; Major sees it as the cross-guard of a sword viewed from above. The lightly sketched monogram in the right foreground recedes and adds depth to the picture.

29

Lovers embracing

Pen drawing. $7^{1}/_{8} \times 5^{1}/_{2}$ in. Probably 1514 (Parker). Signed: VG monogram. Part of the drawing has been cut off at the bottom. Windsor Castle. [P. 39; K. 142]

With a keen eye for detail, Graf portrays the somewhat dissolute love-making of the soldier of fortune. Graf's abbreviated rendering of the coquettishly waving plumes gives an added note of comedy to the hungry lover's sentimental advances. This is a delightful parody of the primitive sensuality which was by no means foreign to Graf's own character.

30

Married Couple taking a Walk

Pen sketch. $8^{1}/_{4} \times 6$ in. Dated 1514. Signed: VG monogram. Basle: Öffentliche Kunstsammlung. [K. 50]

Graf's genius for recording momentary impressions was never more evident than in this sketch. We can almost see the expressions of the promenading couple. This is a highly imaginative caricature of the conceited husband, consumed with boredom, while his wife trots along beside him radiating self satisfaction.

On the bottom right-hand corner of the page is an M surmounted by a crown, which appears on two other drawings (Plates 1 and 31). Its meaning is obscure.

31

Invitation

Pen drawing. $8^{3}/_{8} \times 6^{1}/_{8}$ in. Dated 1516. Signed: VG monogram. Basle: Öffentliche Kunstsammlung. [K. 68]

If we were left in any doubt as to the meaning of this drawing, it would be explained by the motto embroidered on the edge of the richly dressed lady's bodice: "ADAM DER WIR(T?)" (Adam the host). Her generous and slightly indecorous gesture of invitation repeats the information. This is one of Graf's favourite themes. In this version he has taken malicious delight in making the actors persons of rank.

On the bottom left-hand corner is a winged M with a crown reversed (Cf. Plate 1).

32

The Soldier's Farewell

Pen drawing. $8^{3}/_{8} \times 6$ in. Dated 1516. Signed: VG monogram. Basle: Öffentliche Kunstsammlung. [K. 64]

Graf was very fond of the juxtaposition of a raw-boned soldier and a plump little woman. She is always the type of woman who seeks a brief love affair rather than a long-standing attachment. She shows little sign of sorrow at leave-taking, utters a few frivolous words and avoids the man's penetrating gaze. In the hook-nosed warrior, whose rich slashed doublet contrasts strangely with the bare left thigh affected by mercenaries, Major sees a portrait of the artist.

33

The returned Soldier and his Wife

Pen drawing. 7 × 5 1/2 in. Probably 1516 or 1517 (Parker). Signed: V G monogram on a tablet. Amsterdam: Rijksmuseum. [P. 2; K. 143]

This is no light assignation, but a serious conversation between a husband and wife. Silently she weighs in her hand the heavy pouch in which he has brought home his wages. He is evidently trying to justify its origin. Her air of worldly wisdom and sorrowful resignation contrasts strikingly with the childishly guilty bearing of the man.

This highly expressive picture is composed with the utmost simplicity; its effect is heightened by the landscape background.

34

Ensign and Woman Camp-follower

Pen drawing. 8 3/8 × 5 3/4 in. Dated 1516. Signed: V G monogram. Basle: Öffentliche Kunstsammlung. [K. 59]

The soldier flaunting his flag is a recurrent theme upon which Graf never tired of inventing variations. Here the strapping young warrior stands with his back to us; his heavy flag is held aloft like a torch so that it beats in the breeze. On his right stands a camp-follower; she wears a kirtle kilted below the hip and carries a pouch and a dagger. Her figure is rather more carefully modelled and shaded than that of the man. In the background, a jagged line suggests the contour of a mountain range, descending steeply to a lake in which a tower and ships are mirrored.

35

A Nobleman and his Lady on Horseback

Pen sketch. 5 5/8 × 6 3/8 in. Circa 1523 (Koegler). Unsigned. Basle: Öffentliche Kunstsammlung. [K. 109]

The unfinished state of this drawing is greatly to be regretted. Until the time of Schwind there is nothing to rival the romantic gaiety of this picture of a knight riding through the forest with his lady behind him.

Nevertheless this accomplished sketch gives us a good idea of the artist's final intention. Unerring observation is here allied with sureness of composition and fine draughtsmanship. The little picture recalls the evidence Graf gave in court in 1524. He testified that he had gone with his wife and some neighbours to attend the consecration of a church in Hiltelingen, on the right bank of the Rhine. After supping in the little castle there and taking wine at the "New Inn", they had set off homewards, "and Bomgarter, with his wife sitting behind him, rode before us" (Major p. 163–164).

36

Nude Woman and Jester

Pen drawing. 7 1/2 × 5 5/8 in. Circa 1516 (Koegler). Signed: V G monogram. Basle: Öffentliche Kunstsammlung. [K. 71]

This unfinished drawing represents a young woman on her way to the bath, being spied upon by an aged jester who walks just behind her trailing a wooden leg. The figures are lightly outlined with a slight suggestion of modelling. The woman wears a barret and bath-shoes with wooden soles. Her hair hangs in a plait and in her hand is a large dressing-comb. Her jewelry consists of a bracelet, a shoulder-chain, and a collar bearing the letters "OCH. MII", from which hangs a pendant with the initial V.

The jester holds up a pair of spectacles the better to observe her charms, while a raven punishes his impudent curiosity by pecking at his eye.

37

Young Woman and old Reprobate

Pen drawing, unfinished. 7 5/8 × 5 1/2 in. Probably 1518 (Koegler). Unsigned. Basle: Öffentliche Kunstsammlung. [K. 80]

In his later years Graf seems to have established the main contours of his drawing before he applied any modelling or shading. He thereby achieved a strong effect of relief, almost like that of an engraving.

We reproduce the only known example of an unfinished drawing of this kind. Although unsigned, the drawing is sufficiently authenticated by its subject and the motto on the hem of the woman's bodice.

38

Soldier of Fortune in the Bed-chamber of a Courtesan

Pen drawing. 12 1/8 × 8 3/4 in. Probably 1514 or 1516 (Koegler), circa 1511 (Major). Signed: V G monogram on a tablet. Dresden: Lahmann Collection. [K. 132]

This drawing of a nude courtesan and her lover is among Graf's best works. Although the female nude is not drawn in Graf's characteristic manner, the whole work is vividly and freshly conceived.

The man has just laid a handful of coins on the table and looks enquiringly at the girl. She answers by clutching his sleeve and holding out a goblet of wine. The lid of the elaborate vessel lies on the table.

The scene is handled in a highly convincing manner and given added point by the mottoes inscribed on the bed: "God give us joy" and "Luck on my side". The bottom left-hand corner bears the monogram on a tablet, and on the right is the unexplained monogram "EW" surmounted by a crown (Cf. text to Plate 82).

39

Jester and Woman Fiddler

Pen drawing. 12 1/8 × 8 1/8 in. Dated 1523. Signed: Dagger monogram on a tablet. Darmstadt: Museum. [P. 11; K. 138]

Graf gave weird vitality to this degraded creature in motley, upon whose cloak he has wickedly drawn the Basle staff. The contrast between the hideous jester who croaks out a song to the strains of the fiddle, and the beauty of the female form as Graf loved to draw it gives to the drawing that element of outlandishness which is characteristic of Graf's imaginings.

40

Dancing Peasants

Pen drawing. Approx. 8 1/4 × 6 in. Dated 1525. Signed: Dagger monogram. Turin: Biblioteca Reale. [K. 126g]

This is one of a series of eleven drawings of dancing peasants made by Graf at the same time as that of the Piper (Plate 41), in 1525.

They were evidently used as designs for woodcuts, since nearly all have the pricked outlines produced by the tracing process employed in Graf's day; their broad cross-hatching confirms this evidence.

This series of peasants was certainly not original, although we cannot say with certainty from whom it was derived. Koegler recalls Holbein's celebrated peasant-frieze in the *Haus zum Tanz* in Basle, and notes unmistakeable similarities with Manuel's woodcuts of genre and theatrical figures (Cf. K. 118).

41

A Piper

Pen drawing. Approx. 7 7/8 × 5 7/8 in. Dated 1525. Signed: Dagger monogram. Paris: Ecole des Beaux-Arts. [P. 29, K. 147]

This homely genre figure is vividly characterised in all the details of a piper's attitude. In an earlier drawing, Graf had represented soldiers playing the flute (Plate 45). In the present drawing, one of his last works, he returned to his old habit of rendering the single figure as realistically as possible. His pen has given to the figure's fluid outline something of the strange lilt of the bagpipes.

The drawing was made to go with the dancing peasants (Cf. Plate 40). The theme was a popular one and Graf's contemporaries drew and engraved innumerable versions of it, which were often accompanied by sprightly mottoes and eventually found their way into books and almanacs.

42

Vivandière and hanging Corpse

Pen drawing. 12 3/4 × 8 5/8 in. Dated 1525. Signed: Dagger monogram. Basle: Öffentliche Kunstsammlung. [K. 114]

The woman who is represented at an advanced stage of pregnancy is nevertheless dressed in the latest fashion. On her way to the edge of the lake to rinse out her pewter tankard and copper cauldron, she passes close by a gibbet on which a corpse hangs. In the serenity of the sun-drenched landscape, the bearer of new life comes face to face with the hideous harvest of death. The picture is inspired by the antithesis of beginning and end, cradle and grave. At the same time, none but a man terribly familiar with the grimmest aspects of life could have set down

the scene with so callous an impartiality or treated it in so naïvely matter-of-fact a manner. The picture points no moral, presents no *memento mori*. Coldly objective, perhaps deliberately ironic, it owes its lasting charm to the penetrating science and expressive power of its draughtsmanship.

43

Woman stabbing herself beside a Lake

Pen drawing. 12 7/8 × 8 3/4 in. Dated 1523. Signed: Dagger monogram. Basle: Öffentliche Kunstsammlung. [K. 113]

A young woman stands on a boulder at the edge of a lake. Turning her despairing gaze heavenward, she plunges a sword into her breast. On the left, a bearded man with rolled-up sleeves and without his doublet, struggles towards her through the water. Holding fast to a tree that rises above the flood, he attempts with loud cries to dissuade her from her desperate purpose. The deliberate style and studied effect of the composition suggest that the scene was not a momentary invention or an illustration, but held for Graf some deep significance. The billowing scroll terminating in ornamental volutes was clearly intended to bear some explanatory inscription.

44

A Council of War

Pen drawing. 11 1/2 × 8 1/2 in. Dated 1515. Signed: VG monogram. Basle: Öffentliche Kunstsammlung. [K. 57]

This drawing chronicles the contemporary scene in highly realistic detail. The group of warriors pressing round their banner is a symbol of concentrated strength. The flashing eyes of the standard-bearer are fixed upon a distant point: his plumes spread like a flame against the dark cloth of the flag. The overlapping contours of the figures are punctuated by their projecting halberds, swords and pikes.

On the raised foreground stand the captain and his lieutenant; the captain wears riding coat and spurred boots, and is giving orders, while his lieutenant, known by his leather jerkin and iron breast-plate, leans on his pike in an attitude of close attention.

The date of the drawing reminds us that Graf fought at Marignano in that very year. Major identifies the standard-bearer as Hans Bär of Basle, one of the Swiss heroes who fell on that famous field.

45

The Flute Serenade

Pen drawing. 8 5/8 × 6 3/8 in. Dated 1523 (drawn in 1522). Signed: Dagger monogram. Basle: Öffentliche Kunstsammlung. [K. 108]

The four warlike flutists brought a New Year message from Urs Graf to his fellow-craftsman, the Basle goldsmith Jörg Schweiger: the scroll coiled round the branch of the tree bears the conventional greeting and the year.

This fine and carefully drawn picture is of interest to students of cultural history both as a New Year card and as a record of contemporary musical instruments. The quartet is played on transverse flutes of various lengths: the bass flute held by the man with his back turned must be almost four feet long. The leather case for the four instruments hangs from the belt of the musician on the extreme right.

46

Recruiting Scene in the Guild Hall

Pen sketch. 8 3/8 × 12 1/2 in. Circa 1523 (Koegler). Unsigned. Basle: Öffentliche Kunstsammlung. [K. 112]

In a spacious Guild Hall, soldiers and citizens are seated together round a table. A haughty soldier of fortune sits astride one end of the bench; he wears leather cap, slashed doublet and a short broad-sword such as was worn by German lansquenets and sometimes carried by the Swiss as a trophy. The hilt of his heavy two-handed sword rests on his knee. The bearded man on his right, armed with long Swiss sword and Swiss dagger, watches him expectantly to see whether he will accept the proposition of the French officer, who sits at the other end of the table. The officer is distinguished by his knight's hat and fashionably cut hair and by the *fleur-de-lis* on his sleeve: he looks across at the mercenary and takes money from the purse at his belt. Two of the citizens are immersed in conversation; a third, a mere yokel, watches the bargaining with a knowing air.

Meanwhile, a serving man, entering with a maid from the right, pours out wine from a piggin in a wide arc. On the left stands a cooler with two pewter jugs for replenishing the piggin.

The idea underlying the picture is symbolised by the jester behind the recruiting officer and the skeleton behind the soldier. The words on the scroll: "I will list awhile to your talk beneath this rose" refer to the large carved rose on the ceiling, but also to the *sub rosa* recruiting, discountenanced by the authorities. The satirical meaning of the drawing is perhaps that Death is the ultimate profiteer on this recruiting business.

Koegler has pointed out that certain of the figures in this scene, especially that of the bearded Swiss with his back turned, must have been derived from the sketch of a guild banquet made by Holbein in 1522, or even more probably from a glass-painting based on the sketch in the Hall of one of the Basle guilds; the waiter pouring out wine accompanied by the maid-servant plays the same part in both compositions.

47

A Battlefield

Pen drawing. 8 1/4 × 12 1/2 in. Dated 1521. Signed: Dagger monogram. Basle: Öffentliche Kunstsammlung. [K. 106]

The clash of massed armies has left in its wake a field strewn with the bodies of men and beasts, here depicted with ruthless vigour and brutal detail in all the postures of agony and death. The battle itself still rages a little farther back and thence right into the distance. The serried lines of swords and spears in the middle distance suggest the tense collision of a battle still at its height. From this scene of devastation, the eye is led past two corpses hanging from trees to the peaceful lake-landscape in the right background.

The representation is in the nature of a chronicle, intended to record the battle in all its phases. Only the towering figure

of the avidly drinking soldier in the left foreground lends the note of immediacy which experience alone could have supplied.

The same horsemen in the peculiar tall hats appear in a drawing by Niklaus Manuel (Cf. P. Ganz, *Zwei Schreibbüchlein des Niklaus Manuel Deutsch*, Berlin, 1909, Plate 8) in which they are also represented as charging a line of pikemen (Major).

48

Three Soldiers on Guard

Pen sketch. 11 5/8 × 8 3/8 in. Circa 1520/21 (Koegler). Unsigned. Basle: Öffentliche Kunstsammlung. [K. 95]

Graf observed life and events in their true proportions, as manifestations not only of the universal, the common lot of humanity, but also of the immediate and individual. Here he depicts three soldiers on guard-duty who have been joined by a *vivandière*. In a few strokes of the pen, each member of the group is given individuality: the bearded veteran pompously relates his exploits to an attentive young listener, while the seasoned mercenary, old iniquity in every line of his ape-like profile, waits for the young woman to pour out his drink.

Although the execution of this drawing is that of a mere sketch, its carefully elaborated composition gives it the character of a complete picture. The attitudes of the soldiers are well conceived, the erect figure of the man with the lance happily uniting the two groups.

The landscape background is unrelated to the rest of the picture except as a decorative accessory. Graf was ill-versed in spatial composition and never completely freed himself from the mediaeval convention of linear arrangement. In this drawing, as in many others, the landscape with its lake, town, and mountains is a sort of stage-property taken from the store-house of the artist's imagination and adapted to the special decorative requirements of the scene.

49

Two Women chastising a Monk

Pen drawing. 11 1/8 × 8 1/4 in. Dated 1521. Signed: Dagger monogram. Basle: Öffentliche Kunstsammlung. [K. 100]

With the rage of avenging Furies, the two women have flung themselves upon the monk, probably to punish him for some word of pious contumely. One scratches his face till the blood flows, while her friend belabours him with a bunch of keys. Graf depicts this incident with obvious relish and a varied play of draughtsmanship which contrasts with the banality of the slap-stick subject. The figures of the monk and the women on the right recall those of one of Graf's favourite subjects, "Phyllis riding Aristotle".

50

Saint Anthony

Pen drawing. 7 1/2 × 5 1/4 in. Dated 1512. Signed: VG monogram. Vienna: Albertina. [P. 33]

This peculiar early drawing derives its special interest from the note in the upper right-hand corner in which Graf describes himself as "the Devil's-head who drew this".

On the hem of the saint's habit is the unexplained inscription "A : SICH : VM : DICH : PFA(FF) VON : K..V" (Look about thee priest?—). On his cowl is a T-cross with two bells. Beneath the enormous long-rayed nimbus that encircles the saint's head, is a monogram of the name "ANTONIVS". Here Graf has varied the inevitable lake-and-mountain landscape by the addition of a chapel and a graveyard, and has drawn his monogram in heavy raised characters on the foreground.

The autobiographical note recalls the note on another drawing (Cf. Plate 100), but the purpose and meaning of this drawing remain obscure. Perhaps the note was added to palliate the effect of the intentionally irreverent picture.

51

Hermit and Demon-Apparition

Pen drawing. 8 3/8 × 6 1/8 in. Dated 1512. Signed: V G monogram. Basle: Öffentliche Kunstsammlung. [K. 17]

As the hermit wends his solitary way, his shoulders are suddenly gripped by a horned demon with a wooden leg. The monk carries a crucifix, a rosary, and a hat for collecting alms. His face is hidden by his cowl, from which only the point of his long beard emerges. In the background steep cliffs tower up against a dark and cloudy sky; at the mouth of a gorge, a house and the apse of a church are visible.

This drawing ranks above two others of like character because it shows more careful treatment both of contour and shading. Their purposeless confusion of lines is here replaced by firm cross-hatching, which achieves a strong contrast of light and shade and contributes to the intended gruesome-grotesque effect.

This picture has none of the grim solemnity of a *memento mori*; when Graf drew such scenes it was chiefly from a mischievous desire to point out that even a hermit is not free from human frailty, that avarice and self-seeking lurk beneath the monk's cowl as well as the soldier's bonnet.

52

The wise Virgin

Pen drawing. 11 3/8 × 8 1/4 in. Dated 1513. Signed: V G monogram, Basle: Öffentliche Kunstsammlung. [K. 27]

Graf bestowed much care upon the symbolic figure of the wise virgin, intently guarding her light. Here neither sensuality nor malice sought expression; the artist seems to have been intent upon capturing the beauty of a delicate profile and the peculiar charm of maidenly bearing. A gown with a long train and wide fur-lined sleeves lends grace to the figure. The girl's head is framed by a broad linen band pinned over her hair-net. A sunburst is embroidered on her shoulder, and on her bodice the word "OWEMI" (Woe is me), one of those mottoes which may apply either to the figure depicted or to the artist himself.

53

The Archangel Michael

Pen drawing. 12 3/8 × 8 3/8 in. Dated 1516. Signed: V G monogram. Basle: Öffentliche Kunstsammlung. [K. 73]

The Archangel Michael is performing his office of weighing souls. All the ballast that the little monsters can carry in the shape of millstones and anvils fails to sway the balance in their favour; the soul's good deeds outweigh it.

Graf was apparently unconscious of any disharmony between the archangel's villainous countenance and his high judicial office. Here, as so often in Graf's versions of sacred subjects, the combination of irreconcilable secular and religious conventions produces an incongruous effect.

54

The Martyrdom of Saint Sebastian

Pen drawing. 12 1/2 × 8 3/8 in. Dated 1519. Signed: V G monogram. Basle: Öffentliche Kunstsammlung. [K. 86]

In his pitiless representations of human suffering, Graf withheld no detail however brutal. Seldom did he achieve the intensity of formal expression which alone can raise such drawings above the level of realistic description.

Although this drawing may well be counted among Graf's best works, its expressionist style is by no means typical and represents only one side of his character.

Parker points out the resemblance between the saint's pose and that of Christ in a "Scourging" of the Holbein School. At the same time, the motif is far too common for any direct relationship between the two works to be assumed.

55

Parody of a "Saint George and the Dragon"

Pen sketch. 12 1/2 × 8 5/8 in. Dated 1519. Signed: V G monogram. Basle: Öffentliche Kunstsammlung. [K. 85]

With characteristic unconcern, Graf proclaimed his contempt for the conventional manner of representing the legends of the saints officially sanctioned by the Church. In this case we may even assume that some particular fourteenth century picture of St. George inspired his parody; some such basis is suggested by the special stress laid upon the rider's elegance, upon his slim waist, his mail gauntlets and other accessories which would inevitably have provoked the derision of a realist and veteran of the cut-and-thrust school like Graf. The mock reverence expressed by the airy triple halo could scarcely be surpassed. This subject must have possessed special attraction for Graf, since he treated it, albeit in considerably tamer fashion, on several other occasions (Cf. Plates 74, 80, 111, 119).

56

Beheading of Saint Barbara

Pen drawing. 11 1/2 × 7 3/4 in. Dated 1519. Signed: Dagger monogram. Basle: Öffentliche Kunstsammlung. [K. 82]

This highly finished drawing is superior from more than one point of view to the majority of Graf's designs for woodcuts. Interesting above all is the relation of figures to landscape. This landscape is not merely sensitively drawn but plays a decisive part in the pictorial effect of the drama which is being enacted.

This is perhaps the only composition in which Graf gave the landscape a function more essential than that of a dropscene.

57

The Scourging of Christ

Pen sketch. 7 3/8 × 8 1/4 in. Dated 1520. Signed: VG monogram. Basle: Öffentliche Kunstsammlung. [K. 88]

The whole scene is hastily sketched; only the figures of Christ and of the two executioners on the right are drawn in greater detail and with a certain amount of cross-hatching.

Christ has fallen at the foot of the pillar, the rope which held him up having snapped during the scourging. In spite of this, his savage executioners continue to scourge him with whips and rods and to tear his hair. Graf almost overstepped the bounds of decency in thus depicting brutal sadism let loose upon a defenceless victim.

58

Christ taken Prisoner

Pen drawing. 8 1/4 × 5 in. Dated 1521. Signed: Dagger monogram. Basle: Öffentliche Kunstsammlung. [K. 99]

The wildly agitated scene of Christ's capture takes place at the foot of a wooded crag. Christ, already bound, is being dragged away even before he can receive the traitor's kiss. Equally unconventional is the grimace of unholy glee with which Peter falls upon the servant of the high priest. The sickle moon seems to blaze upon the whole scene with the intensity of daylight. The drawing is obviously a design for a woodcut in which Graf brought all his power of dramatic expression into play in order to put the Bible scene into lively popular idiom.

59

Christ, the Man of Sorrows

Charcoal and wash drawing on yellowish-brown paper, heightened with white chalk. 17 1/2 × 14 1/2 in. Dated 1525. Signed: Dagger monogram. Basle: Öffentliche Kunstsammlung. [K. 119]

This drawing, for which the pen-draughtsman used the unaccustomed medium of charcoal and chalk, depicts the Man of Sorrows with an intensity of feeling seldom encountered in Graf's work. The soft chalk is used with perfect mastery; halftones and high-lights are applied with science. The drawing cannot be denied a certain grandeur, although the incongruous note struck by the elaborate calligraphic signature and date detracts somewhat from its artistic value.

It is usual for draughtsmen to prefer charcoal and chalk to the pen in their later work; it need not surprise us to find that Graf conformed to this rule.

60

Bacchante

Pen drawing. 6 3/4 × 6 in. Dated 1517. Signed: V G monogram. Basle: Öffentliche Kunstsammlung. [K. 75]

Graf's work was largely free from the weight of classical myth and all-pervading allegory that encumbered his contemporaries. When he did embark upon such themes, the result was a strange mixture of imperfectly assimilated classical lore and original pictorial conceptions. It would therefore be idle to speculate as to whether this dancing woman, emptying a huge wine-goblet, was meant to be Pandora or merely a bacchante. Graf was content when he had expressed the lavish curves and graceful rhythmic movement of his imaginary dancer.

61

Female Satyr blowing a Horn

Pen drawing. 8 3/8 × 5 7/8 in. Circa 1511/12 (Koegler). Unsigned. Basle: Öffentliche Kunstsammlung. [K. 12]

A nude female satyr with short curly hair, horns, and pointed ears marches along blowing with all her might into a horn (bucina) of fantastic size. She is rigged out in a necklace, a girdle, sandals, and one garter.

Both the style and the subject of this unsigned drawing characterise it as the work of Graf: the deftly controlled line, the stressed right contour of the figure, the typical treatment of a mythical creature, to whom Graf has given the heavily voluptuous form of all his female figures.

62

Young Satyr and Child

Pen drawing. 8 3/8 × 5 7/8 in. Circa 1511 (Parker), probably 1513 (Koegler). Signed: V G monogram and borax box. Basle: Öffentliche Kunstsammlung. [K. 25]

The symbolism of the picture of a satyr holding a champfrein shield, and with a child astride his shoulders, is obscure, but we may assume that Graf, who often wrote in cipher, also attached some secret meaning to this drawing. Hieroglyphic writing, both phonetic and ideographic, had been developed by the Humanists into a science, whose influence finds its clearest record in the emblems adopted by printers. In his intercourse with Basle printers, Graf must have acquired at least a rudimentary knowledge of these signs.

The emphasis laid upon the right-hand contour of the figure is a characteristic legacy of Graf's training as a designer for goldsmiths. Like the borax box, it is a feature of his early work, although it is occasionally found in drawings of a later date.

63

Demon of Love with the four Elements

Pen drawing. 10 1/2 × 8 1/8 in. Probably 1521 (Koegler). Signed: Dagger monogram. Basle: Öffentliche Kunstsammlung. [K.105]

A nude male figure holds aloft with his right hand a globe inscribed with the entwined and crowned initials M H and surrounds it with a cloud of steam that issues from his mouth. A Swiss dagger and a purse hang from the waving riband he wears in lieu of a belt; his left hand grasps a round buckler, and his left foot rests lightly upon a second globe bearing the artist's monogram.

Koegler believes that this drawing represents "a jealous demon of passion, who treads underfoot the symbol of the scorned lover Urs, while exalting that of his beloved to the clouds". According to Major's interpretation, the demon's breath, the burning houses, the lake and the shore, each of which bears an undeciphered inscription, represent the four elements of earth, air, fire, and water. The meaning of the drawing must remain uncertain until the four mottoes have been deciphered. The four elements and their mottoes may possibly refer to the inseparability of the lovers, who cannot exist apart.

64

Fortuna floating on a Lake

Pen drawing. 12 1/2 × 8 5/8 in. Circa 1516 (Koegler). Signed: VG monogram. Basle: Öffentliche Kunstsammlung. [K. 69]

It would be idle to attempt to discover what symbolic meaning Graf attached to this beautiful female figure; she might equally well represent victory, love, joyous living, or indeed the fulfilment of human desire itself.

The sensual appeal of the drawing is enhanced by the unusually subtle interpretation of visual nuances: we feel the airy spaciousness of the landscape and mirror-like surface of the lake. This representation of the human figure in a landscape gives direct and intensely personal expression to a pantheistic feeling for nature of which Graf himself may or may not have been aware.

65

Venus riding on the Clouds

Pen drawing. 7 × 6 in. Circa 1521 (Parker). Signed: Dagger monogram. Nuremberg: Germanisches Museum. [P. 22; K. 135]

Obedient only to the dictates of his sensual fancy, Graf dismissed as mere decorative niceties all such attributes of his goddess as could not serve to heighten the effect of her seductive pose. The main accent is laid upon the lascivious play of her skirt, the rhythmic motion of her sinuous body and the meaningful little demon on her uplifted incense-burner.

66

Fortuna with a Phial

Pen and wash drawing on grey-tinted paper, heightened with white. 10 3/8 × 7 5/8 in. Circa 1520 (Major). Unsigned. Basle: Öffentliche Kunstsammlung.

The subject of this drawing was taken from the Venetian tarot cards (tarocchi) on which various allegorical figures appear. The *Primo Mobile* here represented has a special value in the pack.

Graf has transformed her globe, symbol of the universe, into an alchemist's phial which her fingers grip as if it were a pair of bellows; he seems to have been chiefly interested in the prancing movement of the figure.

The details of this unsigned drawing, which are echoed in many of Graf's works, furnish ample evidence of authorship. The same figure and the same head appear in several of his drawings (Cf. Plates 22, 122), as does the barret as a frame to the head (Cf. Plates 65 and 121). The resemblance between this figure and that of the *Young Woman stepping into the Water* (Plate 23) is particularly striking: the structure of breast and shoulder in the two figures is identical. The treatment of the cast shadow is also characteristic (Cf. Plate 121). Above all the boisterous movement of the figure proclaims its author so conclusively that I have no hesitation in ascribing to Graf a work hitherto given to Manuel (Lucie Stumm, *Niklaus Manuel Deutsch*, Berne 1925, Plate XXIV).

67

Arms of the Soleure Blacksmiths' Guild

Pen and light wash. 11 7/8 × 7 7/8 in. 1509 (Major, Koegler). Signed: VG monogram and borax box. Soleure: Museum. [P. 32; K. 129]

Graf's native town possesses only one of his drawings, this title-page to the statutes of the Soleure Blacksmiths' Guild. He designed it on the occasion of his sojourn there in 1509. The escutcheon of the Guild, a crowned fire-breathing serpent between hammer and tongs, is supported by two wild men: the elder, bearded man carries the red and white standard of Soleure, the younger, the banner of the Guild.

The awkwardness of the composition, the sloping foreground, and the timid stance of the supporters (copied from Schongauer) show the drawing to be an early work. The inscription beside the monogram and borax box, *genad dir gott* (God have mercy on thee), surmounted by a cross, was added by another hand, probably after Graf's death in 1528.

68

Centaur with a Woman and Child

Pen drawing. 11 3/4 × 8 3/8 in. Dated 1513. Signed: VG monogram on a tablet. Basle: Öffentliche Kunstsammlung. [K. 24]

In this simple triangular composition Graf successfully related the mighty figure of the centaur to that of the fashionably dressed lady and at the same time conveyed their tender relationship with a certain blunt delicacy. The bearded centaur wears a garland of leaves on his head; from his right hand hangs a tablet bearing Graf's monogram, while with his left he raises a magnificent Renaissance goblet high above the head of the woman, who sits above him on a grassy bank.

Though the drawing is technically flawless, Graf's treatment of the subject is somewhat colourless and the allegory remains obscure. The drawing acquires biographical interest in the light of Major's suggestion that Graf's wife Sibylla was the model for the female figure.

69

A Satyr, a nude Woman and a slain Man

Pen drawing. 11 1/2 × 8 1/4 in. Dated 1513. Signed: VG monogram. Basle: Öffentliche Kunstsammlung. [K. 21]

Graf's drawings can nearly always be relied upon to puzzle or amuse us. This drawing naïvely reflects a popular conception of humanist philosophy, and conveys the strange mingling of paganism with boisterous sensuality in a pictorial form which is both lively and unusual.

The inscription (of which each word is written in reverse) reads: "IVBITER · ICH · OPFER · DIR · DAS · DV · DAS WIBLI · LOSEST · MIR" (Thus do I sacrifice unto thee Jove that thou mayest this wench unto me give). At the foot of Jupiter's pedestal lies the satyr's vanquished rival (his attitude reminiscent of Peter Flötner's human sundial). The victor clinches the bargain by flinging a handful of coins to the god, while the *Wibli* standing shamefacedly by his side also seems to regard her fate as sealed.

Graf sketched this original scene with the verve and spontaneity born of technical skill and a lively imagination.

70

Aristotle and Phyllis

Pen drawing. 11 1/4 × 8 1/4 in. Dated 1521. Signed: Dagger monogram on a tablet. Dessau: Anhaltische Behördenbibliothek. [P.14]

The philosopher Aristotle is crawling on hands and knees while Phyllis, mounted on his back, brandishes a flail.

This was a late mediaeval story, intended to show that, for all his wisdom, the aged philosopher fell a victim to his foolish love for a young woman because he lacked the true—namely the Christian—code of morality. Needless to say, the delicate lady of the early Gothic pictures has turned into a coarse unbridled baggage, and Graf has done his utmost to stress the grotesqueness of the situation. In contrast with his extremely buxom rider, the lean bridled philosopher looks doubly ridiculous: and it was surely not without satirical intent that Graf perched a bald-headed bird on the tree above his head. Graf also made an etching of this subject (Plate 122), but it lacks the zest and triumphant freedom of the drawing.

71

Pyramus and Thisbe

Pen drawing. 11 1/2 × 8 in. Dated 1525. Signed: Dagger monogram. Basle: Öffentliche Kunstsammlung. [K. 116]

Graf regarded the tragic history of the lovers Pyramus and Thisbe in the light of a farce, and the impudent jester who looks down upon the scene, pretending to be a fountain-statue, expresses his attitude clearly enough. Ovid relates that Pyramus killed himself because he believed Thisbe to be dead, that Thisbe found him and stabbed herself upon her lover's corpse.

Graf's contemporaries had often depicted the scene; he took it upon himself to reveal its lighter side. He deftly parodied the distorted features of the dead warrior, the graceful pose of the heroine piercing her breast with the dagger.

The monumental fountain and the gnarled tree give balance to the composition, and colour is lent by the sharp contrast of light and shade in the foliage and cloudy sky.

72

Castle on a Crag

Pen drawing. 8 3/8 × 6 1/4 in. Dated 1514. Signed: VG monogram. Basle: Öffentliche Kunstsammlung. [K. 53]

Graf's work shows little trace of the romantic feeling for nature which was characteristic of the late Gothic period. Landscape held no personal meaning for him. On the rare occasions when he attempted a landscape composition, he evidently felt the need to dwell upon some feature which could be rendered objectively—in this case, upon the castle. In his impatience of what did not interest him, he allowed his structural analysis of the crag to degenerate into a confusion of arbitrary hatching, and did not even attempt to render the spatial relation of lake to shore. Whether we put this treatment down to clumsiness or caprice, it is responsible for the fantastic element to which the drawing owes its peculiar charm.

73

Little Town on the Shore of a Lake

Pen sketch. 6 1/4 × 8 1/2 in. Dated 1514. Signed: VG monogram. Basle: Öffentliche Kunstsammlung. [K. 49]

This charming sketch and the fantastic drawing of the castle (Plate 72) are the only pure landscapes that Graf is known to have drawn. The subject is of special interest as it is the prototype of the lakeside town so often used by Graf as a background to his figure-compositions. It has not been possible to identify the little township, and we can safely assume that its topography, like that of the castle-landscape, was imaginary.

74

Saint George and the Dragon

Oil on wood, *grisaille* strengthened with black line; blue ground. 23 7/8 × 20 1/2 in. Circa 1520. Unsigned. Basle: Öffentliche Kunstsammlung. [K. 149]

This picture has always been associated with the work of Urs Graf. At first considered as a copy after Graf by Hans Bock, later ascribed to Graf himself, it eventually appeared in the Basle Museum catalogue as "manner of Urs Graf".

If we do not accept Graf's authorship, we have no other alternative than to regard it as the work of a copyist, but what copyist would have reproduced so many characteristic but inessential details of his original?

The helmet, in the shape of a cock, reappears in the *Emperor Maximilian Title-page* (Plate 134); the spiral ornament on the saint's leather jerkin is similar to the tail-piece of the page of calligraphy (Plate 126), while the entwined hearts on the horse's harness also adorn the sleeve of a noble maiden (K. 66). The dragon closely resembles two of Graf's dragons, one on a barret badge (Plate 111), the other in a design for glass-painting (Plate 80). A direct ascription to Graf is also supported by characteristics of draughtsmanship such as the hatching on the tree and the way in which the high-lights are applied. It is also noteworthy that Graf had acquired the technique of *grisaille*-painting in his work on glass.

In any case, no one but Graf would have handled the subject so naïvely, or imagined the scene with such delicious ingenuousness, as if it had never been painted before. No other artist of his day would have had the impudence to omit all but the hindquarters of the horse.

75
War

Oil on parchment. 10 5/8 × 6 3/4 in. Circa 1515. Unsigned. Basle: Öffentliche Kunstsammlung. [K. 148]

As far as we know, Graf worked almost exclusively as a black and white artist; he was essentially a draughtsman. Apart from the *grisaille* (Plate 74), this is the only oil-painting ascribed to him, and as an interesting exception, it is equally worthy of consideration.

In this painting Graf did not venture to depart, either in size or in pictorial organisation, from his normal procedure for a pen drawing, in which he would have depended for colour effect entirely upon the contrast of light and shade.

The central figures of Mars and Bellona poised upon the globe are rather lamely conceived both in pose and gesture. In the lower part of the picture, however, Graf's imagination triumphed in a ghastly fantasy of remarkable power. The figures of the men braced against the wheels of the heavy cannon, and of the falling rider in the foreground, are portrayed with an emotional intensity that suggests some hideous memory of battle behind the nightmare scene.

What Graf withheld in his drawings he expressed in this little oil sketch which far surpasses his only other battle scene (Plate 47) in dramatic power.

76
Urs Graf's Coat of Arms

Design for a glass-painting. Pen and wash drawing. 16 1/2 × 12 3/8 in. Circa 1506 (Koegler), 1511 (Major). Signed: V G monogram on a tablet (bottom right), repeated on a small banner (top right) and borax box (bottom left). Basle: Öffentliche Kunstsammlung. [K. 1]

Urs Graf renounced his family escutcheon and chose as his emblem an angry swan. In this design for a glass-painting, he used the swan's head as a crest. The helmet is borrowed from Dürer's "Arms of Death" (B. 101), the shield from an engraving by Martin Schongauer (B. 98). The elaborate convolutions of the acanthus-like mantling set off the extreme simplicity of shield and helmet. The frame of the escutcheon is half architectural, half vegetal: leafy fruit-bearing branches spring from the tops of the flanking tree-trunks and infants disport themselves upon boughs and pilasters.

77
Mercenary and Woman supporting a Shield

Design for a glass-painting. Pen drawing. 9 5/8 × 7 1/4 in. Circa 1511/12 (Koegler). Signed: V G monogram. Basle: Öffentliche Kunstsammlung. [K. 11]

On the right stands a nude woman holding the shield by its strap. Opposite her and facing towards her stands a mercenary armed with sword and dagger and grasping his lance with both hands. This characteristic pose appears in several other drawings and woodcuts. The woman wears a barret, two necklaces, a girdle and a dagger and holds an apple in her left hand. The motto inscribed on the scroll that waves above her head is de-

rived from Seneca's *fatum rotat omnia*. Graf's favourite subject, the soldier and his lass, is here treated in tamer fashion than usual.

The careful disposition and framing of the figures and the lively style of the drawing lead us to assign it to the year 1512, when the experiences of war had not yet deeply affected Graf's style.

78
The Stehelin-Bischoff Arms of Alliance

Design for a glass-painting. Pen drawing. 14 7/8 × 16 1/8 in. Dated 1515. Signed: V G monogram. Basle: Öffentliche Kunstsammlung. [K. 55]

This design for a glass-painting deserves special attention because it combines all the elements of Graf's pictorial repertoire: the nude woman, the jester, standard-bearer and *putti*, the characteristic lake-scene with the reflected ships, the crags, the castles, and the winding causeways, as well as the delicately drawn ornament of foliated scroll, acanthus leaf and slender cornucopia.

The deep shadows that outline the light surfaces of the escutcheons give life and depth to the whole composition. It is interesting to distinguish the parts of the design in which the artist followed his own bent from those in which he merely carried out a meaningless routine.

The escutcheon with the ox belonged to the Basle cloth-merchant Hieronymus Stehelin, the other to his wife, Ottilia Bischoff, also of Basle. As Stehelin was killed at the battle of Marignano in September (13th or 14th) 1515, he probably never saw the glass-painting he had commissioned after this design which was drawn in the year of his death.

79
The Graf-von Brunn Arms of Alliance

Design for a glass-painting. Pen dawing. 12 1/4 × 8 1/2 in. Dated 1518. Inscribed on the scroll: "VRS · GRAF · — S · VON · BRVNN". Basle: Öffentliche Kunstsammlung. [K. 77]

In this design, made for his own use, Graf combined the escutcheon already reproduced (Plate 76) with that of his wife Sibylla von Brunn.

The two shields with their elaborate crests were placed so close together that the upper corner of the von Brunn shield had to be curved inwards to gain space. Beside it stands the graceful figure of Sibylla as supporter. She is richly dressed and an elegant plumed barret frames her braided hair.

The structure of the framing niche is architecturally impossible and does not even contribute to the decorative effect.

80
Saint George and the Dragon

Design for a glass-painting. Pen and wash drawing: line and tint both greenish-yellow. 9 × 8 1/4 in. Diameter of the drawing: 8 in. Dated 1521. Signed: Dagger monogram. Basle: Öffentliche Kunstsammlung. [K. 102]

Saint George, mounted on a prancing steed, raises his sword to deal the death-blow to the monster which lies beneath him, already transfixed by his spear. On the saint's breastplate is a pious invocation to the Virgin.

Graf was repeatedly called upon to draw this subject (Cf. Plates 55, 74, 111, 119) which was a favourite in all branches of representative art. Goldsmiths in particular often decorated silver pendants and barret-brooches with the images of St. George and St. Christopher. Nevertheless such warlike subjects are comparatively rare in Graf's work, and surprisingly so when we consider how much fighting of every kind he must have seen.

The particular size and colour and the circular frame of this drawing show it to be a design for a glass painting intended for a monolith pane (Major). Graf made three other circular wash drawings of the same type and size in 1521: St. Christopher in red, St. Catherine in blue, and the Holy Family in yellowish-brown wash [K. 104, 101, 103].

81

Putto blowing a Horn

Fragment of a glass-painting; *grisaille* heightened with yellow. 3 1/2 × 5 1/2 in. Circa 1515 (Major). Unsigned. Basle: Historisches Museum: No. 1930, 622.

Graf must have designed a considerable number of glass-paintings which are now lost to us. Among the few which survive and seem to bear a direct relation to Graf's known work is this fragment in the Basle Historical Museum representing a *putto* seated on a capital blowing a horn. Graf's style is clearly recognisable in the fragments of ornamental foliage which present a typical combination of Gothic and Renaissance elements. No less characteristic is the structure of the frame, its architectural and organic elements linked by the corner figure of the *putto*.

82

Woman supporting a Shield

Fragment of a glass-painting. 7 3/8 × 5 3/8 in. 1511 (Major). Signed: " · VRSVS · GRAF v E W · " Zürich: Schweizerisches Landesmuseum: No. 1830.

The only signed glass-painting which has come down to us is reduced to a mere fragment. It was presented to the National Museum of Switzerland by Professor J.R. Rahn in 1895.

This charming supporter retains her conventional Gothic attitude; she wears a yellow barret on her long golden hair and a yellow gown with a hanging train.

On the hem of her gown and train is painted the artist's signature followed by the initials "v (probably meaning *und*) EW" (and? EW). These initials were assumed at one time to be those of a member of the Wolleb family, since Graf had worked as an apprentice to the glass painter Hans Heinrich Wolleb in Basle in 1511. The opinion is no longer tenable, however, since the initials are repeated not only on the design for a glass painting with the Oesterreich arms dated 1511 by Koegler (K. 10), but on other drawings unconnected with glass painting. These include a drawing of a *putto* probably made in about 1513 (K. 23) and the Solider of Fortune and Courtesan drawing (Plate 38) in which the initials are surmounted by a crown, often used by Graf as an emblem of love (Cf. Plates 1, 3, 30, 31, 63).

83–84

Christ at Supper in the House of Lazarus
Christ's Agony in the Garden

Two glass-paintings after designs by Urs Graf. 16 7/8 × 12 in. 1506/07 Koegler). Unsigned. Basle: *Zscheckenbürlin* Room of the former Carthusian Monastery (now the Orphanage). [K.151]

The design of these glass paintings and of two others depicting *Christ's Entry into Jerusalem* and *Christ taken Prisoner* was first ascribed to Graf by Koegler in 1926. Compared with his woodcuts for Ringmann's *Passion* made in Strasbourg in 1503 (Plate 130), they reveal marked artistic progress; at the same time it is not always easy to distinguish Graf's own ideas from those for which he was indebted to others. The clear composition of the scenes and the fine portrayal of individual figures such as the graceful Magdalen in the foreground of the Supper and the impressive St. Peter sleeping in the Garden suggest that Graf had direct access to excellent versions of his subjects, and perhaps even to large painted panels.

The glass paintings possess a splendid range of colour, whose richness appears especially in the drapery, for instance in the fine contrast between the yellow robe of Judas and the deep blue gown of the Magdalen. In the upper part of the pictures, the deep colour of the Gothic period gives way to the light background and pale blue sky characteristic of the Renaissance. The frames are painted in *grisaille* heightened with yellow.

85

Ostrich Egg Goblet

Design for goldsmith's work. Pen and India ink drawing. 11 7/8 × 6 3/4 in. Circa 1514 (Koegler). Unsigned. Basle: Öffentliche Kunstsammlung. [K. 35]

Graf's creative vitality is apparent even in the execution of this simple piece of decorative design. Although he did not hesitate to use ready-made patterns, and was content to draw the simple acanthus leaf in innumerable variations, this design for a goblet is an artistic achievement because it is governed throughout by a clear formal purpose. Nowhere did he allow ornamental luxuriance to endanger the unity of effect of the completed goblet, and as though to satisfy himself of its final effect, he even gave relief to his design, a useless labour as far as the goldsmith was concerned.

This design was first ascribed to Graf by Koegler in 1926.

86

Jester with a Drum

Design for a dagger-sheath. Pen drawing. 8 3/8 × 2 5/8 in. Scabbard: 8 × 1 7/8 in. The tip has been cut off. Probably 1511 (Koegler), circa 1511/12 (Major). Unsigned. Basle: Öffentliche Kunstsammlung. [K. 9]

The juggler is providing an interesting type of popular entertainment. The vibration of the drum-skin makes his puppets execute grotesque dances to the accompaniment of the pipe. The small shields (bearing the arms of Basle, Soleure, etc.) that adorn his cowl probably show that his entertainment was licensed by the authorities.

28

This design is noteworthy not only for its folk-historical subject, but for the liveliness and breadth of its execution; the leaves and fruit which constitute the main elements of the ornament are drawn with fine economy of effect.

87

Drummer and Fifer

Design for a dagger-sheath. Pen drawing. $8 \times 2\,3/4$ in. Scabbard $7\,5/8 \times 2\,5/8$ in. 1509/10 (Koegler), 1511/12 (Major). Unsigned. Basle: Öffentliche Kunstsammlung. [K. 7]

This fundamentally simple but well composed drawing owes its charm to the figures of the drummer and fifer. Although their poses betray the uncertainty characteristic of Graf's early figures, this is more than redeemed by the liveliness of the whole picture and by that fact that he has here depicted the very music-makers of sixteenth-century Basle.

88–89

A Skirmish between Swiss and German Mercenaries

Niello of a scabbard. $18\,1/4 \times 1\,3/4$ in. 1515/17 (Major). Unsigned. Upper half: Berlin: Kupferstichkabinett. Lower half: Basle: Öffentliche Kunstsammlung. [Koegler, Beiträge No. 33, and His 19]

Graf delighted in a fight and so he decorated this scabbard with characteristic zest.

It was evidently intended for a Swiss sword, and the Swiss, needless to say, are getting the upper hand in a fight with German lansquenets. Their triumph is proclaimed by the figure of the standard-bearer whose banner carries the emblems of the Swiss free-lancers. Two duels are going on. The first duel celebrates the courage of the Switzer who, undaunted by his opponent's sword, grips him by the feet; the second shows the miserable defeat of the lansquenet whose terror of the Swiss pike is writ large upon his countenance. He has lost his balance, and, hanging from a branch, forms the tip of the design.

All Graf's scabbard designs have a vertical arrangement. Whereas Holbein usually composed his picture horizontally, Graf's exclusive gift for portraying single figures led him to prefer a vertical sequence or the tapering ascent of the Gothic style. This arrangement allowed him to draw his figures on a larger scale.

The subdivision of the weapon was defined by Holbein in the repartition of his design. Graf solved the problem by using his foliated scroll as a scaffolding for the vertical disposition of the figures.

This niello-proof is one of the best of all Graf's designs of this kind known to us.

90

Roman Soldier

Niello of a dagger-sheath. $9\,1/2 \times 1\,1/8$ in. 1512 (Major). Signed: V G monogram on a shield. Basle: Öffentliche Kunstsammlung. [His 18]

The floral form of volute that predominates in this design fulfils the purpose of decoration better than the baluster-like elements on which some of the other designs are based.

Again, in this warrior's pose, we note the characteristic elegantly advanced leg, drawn this time in profile. His trophies and the champfrein shape of his shield together with other stylistic features lead us to date the design as circa 1512.

91

Eight Putti climbing a Spray

Niello of a dagger-sheath. 7×2 in. 1513 (Major). Signed: V G monogram on a tablet. Basle: Öffentliche Kunstsammlung. [His 14]

With this design Graf's sparkling fancy created a gem of Basle workmanship. Naturally the niello-proof cannot give an adequate idea of the original, but a closer study even of the proof reveals the astonishing variety here achieved with the simplest of motifs. The foliated scroll curls in a triple widening spiral, each curve enclosing fruit or blossom, its stem a ladder for the antics of pretty cherubs and gambolling children.

The raised white areas of the niello-proof show that the design was embossed. This signed work is clear evidence of Graf's fertile invention and of his special gift for floral design: it owes its unique liveliness to the perfect interplay of formal elements and well-drawn figures.

92

Putto with a Monogram-tablet

Niello of a dagger-sheath. $6\,1/2 \times 7/8$ in. Dated 1512. Signed: V G monogram. Basle: Öffentliche Kunstsammlung. [His 17]

Its lucid combination of decorative elements places this design above all Graf's other work in this field. Major suggests that he closely followed or even directly copied an Italian design.

93

Five Putti playing with Hoops

Design for a scabbard. Pen drawing. $12\,5/8 \times 2\,1/4$ in. Scabbard: $12\,1/2 \times 1\,1/2$ in. 1513 (Major), circa 1514 (Koegler). Unsigned. Basle: Öffentliche Kunstsammlung. [K. 37]

The bodies of the putti dominate this design, while the knotted spiral stem upon which they play with their hoops serves only as a scaffolding. Each link in this well-developed sequence is richly varied in detail, yet clearly related to its neighbour. The basic simplicity of the design suggests that Graf had the requirements of the embosser in mind.

94

Cupid and Bow

Niello of a scabbard. Total length: $18\,1/2 \times 1\,3/4$ in Only the upper half is reproduced. 1515/17 (Major). Unsigned. Berlin: Kupferstichkabinett. [Koegler, Beiträge No. 31]

In this comparatively late work Graf used elements characteristic of Renaissance ornament in a rather looser sequence and paid more attention to the shape of individual elements. He laid stress upon the cup and vase-like elements of the design by attempting to reproduce their curved surfaces. Thus the design itself and the chubby cupid who crowns it are equally characteristic of Graf's original style. In response to his talent for expressing individual form, he neglected the requirements of sequence and composition; at any moment a sudden inventive whim might prompt him to jeopardise the unity of his effect.

95

Nude Woman wearing a Barret

Niello of a dagger-sheath. 8 3/8 × 2 in. 1512 (Major). Unsigned. Basle: Öffentliche Kunstsammlung. [His 15]

Unlike the male figures and *putti* that decorate Graf's weapons, the female figures were always supplied with a scroll which on the finished scabbard was to bear a name or motto.

In this design, Graf's earliest known work of the kind, the living curve of the stem is skilfully echoed in the streaming lines of the scroll which frames the figure.

96

Female Nude with braided Hair

Niello of a dagger-sheath 8 × 1 3/4 in. 1514 (Major). Unsigned. Berlin: Kupferstichkabinett. [Koegler, Beiträge No. 30]

The lower half of this sheath bears Renaissance ornament culminating in the head and wings of a cherub.

The stress laid upon the volutes and the careful shading of surfaces which detract from the formal clarity of the Renaissance design are characteristic features of Graf's Gothic style. The female figure, though rather precariously posed, reveals a considerable advance in Graf's rendering of anatomical detail.

Graf again used his wife as a model for this graceful pose. A preliminary study for this *niello* dated 1514 (K. 43) enables us to date it with certainty.

97

Female Nude with a Monogram

Niello of a dagger-sheath. 7 3/8 × 1 1/4 in. 1515/16 (Major). Signed: V G monogram. Basle: Öffentliche Kunstsammlung. [His 16]

When we compare this design with Graf's earliest known dagger-sheath of the same type (Plate 95), we can appreciate the result of artistic experience and ceaseless endeavour.

Graf has given new sharpness of relief to his foliated scroll, new vigour to its upward growth: the plain scroll is simplified the better to set off the female figure, whose modelling is now directly governed by the sure lines of the contour.

The outstretched leg was clearly intended to enhance the coquettish grace of this pose, although it is a feature of all German art from 1480 onwards. A late-fifteenth-century dance step is believed to have contributed to the widespread popularity of the pose.

98–99

Female Nude on a Lute
Rose-bearing foliated Scroll

Design for a knife-sheath. Design for obverse: Pen and brown wash drawing. 6 1/8 × 2 in. Design for reverse: Pen drawing. 6 1/8 × 2 in. Sheath: 5 7/8 × 1 1/2 and 5 7/8 × 1 1/2 in. Circa 1514 (Koegler), 1514 (Major). Unsigned. Basle: Öffentliche Kunstsammlung. [K. 33 and 34]

To decorate the obverse of his sheath Graf drew the delightfully natural pose of a young woman brushing out her long hair with one of the tufted bristle brushes of the period; the nude figure stands gracefully upon a lute. Scroll and Renaissance leaf ornament complete the design.

A spiral rose-bearing stem was to adorn the reverse of the sheath; its light yet rhythmic interlacings reveal a fine feeling for design. This drawing was at one time in the Hans Holbein the Younger Sketchbook until it was recognised by Major as the reverse side of this sheath. Its border corresponds in size and shape with that of the obverse design, which was heightened with wash because it was intended to be embossed, whereas the reverse was to be chased. Many of the Renaissance dagger- and knife-sheaths which have come down to us display this combination of raised ornament either hammered or cast in silver on the obverse, and simple chased design on the reverse.

The *frawen parmesser* or lady's table-knife was worn in a sheath which hung from her girdle on a thin chain or strap known as the *Porte*. Major suggests that Graf designed this sheath for his wife, whose figure it depicts.

100

Virgin and Child

Design for a monstrance-statuette. Pen drawing. 9 5/8 × 3 3/8 in. Height of the figure: 4 1/2 in. Dated 1518. Signed: V G monogram above a Swiss dagger. Basle: Öffentliche Kunstsammlung. [K. 78]

The figure of the Virgin, represented as Queen of Heaven, stands on a hastily sketched Gothic bracket. Here Graf has again used his favourite pose of bent knee and outswung hip. The carefully defined folds of the drapery and the economy with which relief is indicated show that the drawing was a goldsmith's design.

The Virgin wears a rather ill-fitting crown and the Child's triple halo is still pierced by its governing lines. Graf's Madonna has all the air of a contented bourgeoise. The similarity of her pose with that of Sibylla von Brunn in the 1518 drawing (Plate 79) leads Major to suggest that this is another portrait of Graf's young wife. Beneath the date, monogram and dagger is an ironic little rhyme written in Graf's own characters: *Vrsüs Graff, Daz tültig schaff* (Ursus Graf, the patient sheep).

101–104

Four Putti: Two playing with Vessels,
One playing the Flute, the fourth a Cupid

Nielli of barret-brooches. 1 1/4 in. in diameter. Circa 1513/14. Unsigned. Berlin: Kupferstichkabinett. [Koegler, Beiträge No. 34a–d]

These charming medallions formed part of Basilius Amerbach's collection and appear in his catalogue, compiled in 1580. They were not associated with Graf's work, however, until Koegler rightly ascribed them to him in 1907, dating them 1513/14.

Major discovered a clue to their dating in a processional cross belonging to the Catholic Church of Offenburg, on which copies of these designs appear with but slight variations. As the year 1515 is engraved on the cross, the four medallions must have been designed before that date, that is in about 1513/14. This evidence confirms the date originally suggested by Koegler.

(Cf. Koegler, *Zwei Kupferstiche und eine Zeichnung von Urs Graf*, *Anzeiger für Schweizerische Altertumskunde*, 1930, p. 38 et seq. in which the four medallions are reproduced and dated 1515/17. The processional cross is reproduced in: Max Wingenroth, *Die Kunstdenkmäler des Kreises Offenburg*, Tübingen 1908, Plate XVI and fig. 269.)

105

Steinmetz-Holzach Arms of Alliance

Niello of a barret-brooch. 2 1/4 in. in diameter. Dated 1521. Unsigned. Berlin: Kupferstichkabinett.

This medallion whose supporter embraces the shields of the Steinmetz family (scabbling pick) and of the Holzach family (lion rampant) of Basle was first ascribed to Graf by Koegler in 1930 *(Anzeiger für Schweizerische Altertumskunde*, 1930, p. 41). Since the only marriage between the Steinmetz-Holzach families of which we know took place in the fifteenth century, the *niello* was probably commissioned by some pious descendant of the marriage in honour of his forebears.

Heinrich Steinmetz, merchant and member of the Basle Council (1423–78, died 1488) took as his second wife Brida Holzach (1446–88). Graf's client may have been Magister Niklaus Steinmetz, member of the Chapter of St. Peter's, Basle, who bequeathed his property to his Holzach cousins in 1524. Graf's solution of this problem of heraldic design is equally successful from the artistic point of view. The pert young supporter lends decided character as well as unity to the design.

106–107

Putto on a Globe holding a Branch
Putto on a Globe holding a Distaff

Nielli of barret-brooches. Oval: 2 1/4 × 1 1/2 in. Dated 1513 and 1514 respectively. Basle: Öffentliche Kunstsammlung, Hamburg: Kunsthalle. [His 13; Koegler, Beiträge No. 29]

Considered side by side, these two closely related designs give a good idea of the variety of effect that Graf achieved within the same limits of frame and motif. In the earlier work the rather loosely constructed figure of the *putto* seems to stand out from the frame, giving a cameo-like effect. A year later, with the larger and better constructed figure, Graf achieved a fuller pictorial effect, without sacrificing the decorative unity of his design. These stylistic differences are of strictly relative value, since the special quality of each design is inseparable from its style.

108

Saint Christopher

Niello of a barret-brooch. 2 3/4 in. in diameter. 1513 (Major). Signed: VG monogram on a tablet. Basle: Öffentliche Kunstsammlung. [His 12]

A sketch for this picture of the sturdily striding St.Christopher (Plate 111, No. 9) gives evidence of the marked degree to which Graf was influenced by the traditional conception of the subjects he treated. The clarity of the drawing was lost in the chasing, since Graf not only could not resist adding a landscape background, but wielded the burin with too heavy a hand. The movement of the figure, however, is rendered with the detailed precision of a skilled goldsmith and the infant Christ is given a new and graceful pose.

109–110

Saint Christopher—The young Tobias

Nielli (obverse and reverse) of a pendant. 2 1/2 in. in diameter. 1511/12 (Major). Signed: VG monogram and borax box. Basle: Öffentliche Kunstsammlung. [His 11 and 10]

The relationship between its two themes, both symbolic of the protection of the traveller, suggests that this medal was intended as an amulet. The obverse shows St. Christopher about to carry the infant Jesus across the river. On the reverse is the Archangel Raphael reassuring young Tobias who has been frightened by the appearance of a monstrous fish. In the background, supposedly at a great distance, stands Raguel's house in Ecbatana towards which the travellers are journeying. There too Raphael acts as Tobias' guardian by putting to flight three monsters with his sword.

This simultaneous presentation of two scenes which were actually separated by time is a survival of mediaeval tradition. That these are early works is demonstrated not only by the borax box signature, but also by the rather uncertain treatment of the figures.

111

Twelve Designs for Barret-Brooches

Pen drawings. 8 1/2 × 12 3/8 in. 1513 (Major), probably 1512 (Koegler). Unsigned. Basle: Öffentliche Kunstsammlung. [K.15]

1. St.Barbara: Diameter 2 1/4 in. - 2. St.Catherine: Diameter 2 1/4 in. - 3. St.Mary Magdalen: Diameter 2 1/4 in. - 4. St.Veronica: Diameter 2 1/4 in. - 5. St.Sebastian: 2 1/2 × 1 3/8 in. - 6. St.John the Baptist: 2 1/2 × 1 3/8 in. - 7. St.George on Foot: 2 3/4 × 1 5/8 in. - 8. St.George on Horseback: Diameter 2 1/4 in. - 9. St.Christopher: Diameter 2 1/4 in. - 10.Virgin and Child: 2 1/2 × 1 1/2 in. - 11. St.Ulric: 2 1/4 × 1 3/8 in. - 12.The Annunciation: Diameter 2 1/4 in.

Even in these little pictures of saints, Graf found scope for his originality. Religious subjects inspired some of his most delightful formal conceptions, among them the effective poses of the female saints Nos. 1–3. There is a close relationship between these figures and that of the seated woman in the drawing dated 1513 (Plate 68). Major has shown that Graf used a much simplified version of this *St.Veronica* (No. 4) as a design for a woodcut (Cf. *Basler Zeitschr. f. Geschichte und Altertums-*

kunde X, 1911, p. 415/17). On the other hand the *St. Sebastian* (No. 5) is clearly based on the study of a *Nude Youth* (Plate 11).

Some idea of the effect of the finished barret-brooches, for which these designs were mainly used, is given by the *niello-print* (Plate 108) of a chased design based on the St. Christopher (No. 9). Unlike the St. Veronica woodcut, the St. Christopher chased design is an elaboration of the drawing on which it was based; in thus enriching his design, Graf maintained a clear relationship between its decorative and pictorial elements.

112

Seal with the Rordorf Escutcheon

Lead cast from a seal. Diameter: 5/8 in. Circa 1515 (Major). Unsigned. Basle: Historisches Museum, No. 1918. 224. From the collection of Basilius Amerbach of Basle (1533–1591).

This cast, bearing the escutcheon of the Rordorf family of Zurich with a *putto* as supporter and the initials I. R., was made from a seal ascribed to Graf by Major. The seal was made for the Junker Jakob Rordorf (died 1556), whose mother Anna was a Holzach of Basle. Possibly her father Eucharius Holzach, Chief Magistrate and member of the Goldsmiths' Guild in Basle (died 1521), may have commissioned his fellow-guildsman Urs Graf to make the seal for his grandson Jakob Rordorf of Zurich.

The design of the seal is developed in skilful response to its circular frame. The curve of the frame merges into the base of the shield, which in turn forms the connecting link with the spiral form of the charge, while the graceful figure of the child with outstretched arms resolves the circular theme and gives the dominant note to the design.

113–115

Silver Coinage of the City of Basle

Diameter: 1 1/8 in. Late 1519 (Major). Unsigned.

113. Obverse: *Virgin and Child* (half-length) surrounded by inscription (Gothic capitals): " · AVE : MARIA : GRACIA : PL(ENA)". Ex. Basle: Historisches Museum, No. 1903. 618.
[Ewig, *Münzkatalog*, No. 323]

114. Reverse of 113. *Basle Staff in a Triglyph* surrounded by inscription (Gothic capitals): "+MONETA : BASILIENSIS : 1520"
115. Obverse: *Virgin and Child* (full-length) surrounded by inscription (Gothic capitals): " · AVE : MARIA : GRACIA : PL(ENA)". Ex. Basle: Historisches Museum, No. 1903. 622.
[Ewig, *Münzkatalog*, No. 325]

Urs Graf also worked as a die-cutter. On February 18th, 1520, the Basle Council paid 8 *Pfund*, 15 *Schilling* "for the die for making silver coins to Urs the Goldsmith" (quoted by Major p. 22). His official appointment as Die-cutter to the City of Basle is proof of the confidence placed in his ability as a craftsman and designer. In fact the coins discovered by Major are exceptional both in design and execution. Each design is a masterly solution of the problem of combining type with inscription. It is notable that Graf in his standing Madonna design omitted not only the mandorla but also the crescent moon, hitherto regarded as an indispensable attribute of the subject. His introduction of the half-length Virgin was an innovation that gave a new breadth and scope to the type.

Chased silver Plate from the Reliquary of St. Bernard

3 1/8 × 7 in. 1519. Signed: Dagger monogram. Zurich: Schweizerisches Landesmuseum. [His 27]

The two pictures which decorate this plate are linked by an architectural frame, consisting of two arches and three pillars crowned by leaf ornament.

On the left, Christ bends down from the cross to embrace St. Bernard of Clairvaux. Against the monastery wall which forms the background, leans the shield of the Cistercian order. On the arch is inscribed the explanatory hexameter: "STRINCIT ET HVNC LINGNO CRVCIS REFLEXVS IESVS".

The picture on the right represents the donation of the bust of St. Bernard to the Monastery of St. Urban (Canton of Lucerne) by its Abbot Erhard Kastler. Against the wall beside the shield of the Order leans the abbot's shield. The hexameter is a prayer to St. Bernard asking him to accept the offering.

This silver plate adorned the front of the pedestal bearing the bust of the saint. It is one of eight such plates which Graf designed for the pedestal. Four of them are now in the National Museum in Zurich; the remaining four are in an English private collection.

Graf designed these pictures in simple narrative form. Despite the sketchiness of their composition, these little pictures rank as works of art by virtue of the linear economy with which the traditional character of each personage is conveyed.

Erhard Kastler, Abbot of St. Urban's, depicted as kneeling donor on this plate, commissioned the silver reliquary as a consecration gift on the occasion of the completion of the monastery building in 1519. Two of the plates bear this date, and on the back of the embossed silver bust, which disappeared in 1850, was the full signature: *Ursus Graff von Solotorn 1519*. Graf must therefore have produced this important work (which brought him 237 1/2 gold ducats) during his exile in Soleure, where he probably made use of his father's workshop.

(On the subject of the Reliquary of St. Bernard cf. Major p. 111–123.)

117

Shooting Cupids—Eve and the Serpent

Stamped leather work. Unsigned. Binding of Erasmus: *Paraclesis*, Basle, Joh. Froben, 1519, from the library of Bonifacius Amerbach of Basle (1495–1562). Reddish-brown leather: gilding on central panel.

Cupid panels: 4 1/2 × 3/4 in. 1513 (Major). Eve panels: 4 1/4 × 1/2 in. After 1515 (Major). Basle: Universitätsbibliothek, F. G. VIII². 19.

These designs were stamped by means of a roller matrix, a small metal cylinder on whose casing the design to be stamped was cut.

The ornamental borders with the two shooting cupids are superior in quality to the central panels which are very poorly designed and were copied from woodcut borders designed by Graf in 1515 (His 325,e).

The pearl edging and star pattern of the cupid border and the detailed modelling of the birds (owl and duck) produce the contrast of light and shade essential to this type of leather-decoration. Characteristic details of pose give ample grounds for ascribing these figures to Graf.

118–119
Venus—Saint George and the Dragon

118. Stamped leather work. Unsigned. Binding in Basle State Archives (St.Theodor A.). 4 5/8 × 5/8 in. 1514 (Major).

119. Stamped leather work. Unsigned. Ibid. (Klosterarchiv: Kartause C.). 5 × 5/8 in. Circa 1513 (Major).

His experience in the decoration of dagger-sheaths must have made it easy for Graf to design these roller matrices. The two tasks are related not only by the similarity of the motifs required but by the oblong shape of the design. The disadvantage of these oblong patterns lies in the limited usefulness of the matrices, since they are suitable only for certain formats.

This Venus border is remarkable for the clarity of its ornament and the delicacy of its modelling. Major identifies this well-proportioned Venus with the pretty rounded face as the artist's wife Sibylla von Brunn (Cf. Plate 20 and especially the female nude of 1514, K. 43).

120
Seated Soldier

Engraving. 4 × 3 in. Dated 1513. Signed: VG monogram. Karlsruhe: Kunsthalle. [His 9; K. 152]

Out of the comparatively small group of engravings by Graf known to us, several were executed after Dürer and Schongauer. This is the only original engraving by Graf that we possess.

In this engraving his technique is so fine, his hatching so dense, that certain details are brought into too sharp a relief. The figure however reveals Graf's gift for analysing a pose. Figure and landscape are well related in this composition whose determining factors are the raised arm grasping the pike, the dark tree-trunk, and the lines of plumes and sword.

121
Young Woman washing her Feet

Etching. 5 1/2 × 2 3/4 in. Dated 1513. Signed: Dagger monogram and Basle staff. Inscription in cipher top right deciphered as: "VRSVS · GRAF · VON · BASEL". Basle: Öffentliche Kunst-sammlung. [His 8; K. 155]

Although this is one of the earliest etchings and is therefore particularly interesting from a technical point of view, it deserves consideration for its high artistic quality alone. In comparison with most of the female figures in Graf's drawings, this young woman seems almost slender, and the natural ease of her pose is expressed in a masterly fashion. The shadow she casts upon the wall—that of an old crone facing the other way—is typical of Graf's satirical touch at its lightest. Although this work was dated by the artist himself, historians do not agree as to the actual date of its execution. Those who accept Graf's date of 1513 assume in consequence that this was one of the earliest

etchings. Koegler opposes this view, pointing out that Graf first made use of his cipher in 1523 (Cf. Plate 126), and calling attention to peculiarities of costume and style that appear in woodcuts and drawings produced soon after 1520. He holds therefore that a false date must have been given deliberately to this work. Either opinion can be defended, although arguments based on style are open to question in the case of an artist whose development was not governed by any inner law. Another argument can be put forward in favour of the earlier date, namely that Graf, both in his early portrait-drawings and in the standard-bearer in white ink of 1514 (Plate 15), already produced work of high quality, and that the problem of cast shadow interested him particularly in those years (Cf. Plates 133 and 141).

122
Aristotle and Phyllis

Etching. 3 1/2 × 3 1/8 in. Dated 1519. Signed: Dagger monogram. Basle: Öffentliche Kunstsammlung. [His 7; K. 154]

The story of Aristotle and Phyllis, an allegory of man's sensual enslavement to woman, is derived from a westernised version of an Indian tale. Its exclusively moral purpose favoured its repetition in picture and sermon, and Renaissance artists were particularly alive to the entertainment value of its somewhat lewd subject. Graf was the last man to let such an opportunity slip.

He used the subject not only in this extremely fine early etching, but in the no less lively drawing in Dessau (Plate 70) of which the drawing reproduced as Plate 49 is a variant. In this small etching Graf makes skilful use of relief, and his gift for ornament found triumphant expression in the fantastic plumed hat of his nude Phyllis.

123–124
Standard-Bearers of Lucerne and Valais

White-on-black woodcuts. Monotypes. 7 1/2 × 4 1/4 in. 1521. Some of the prints of this series are signed with the dagger monogram and dated. Ex. Aarau: Kantonale Sammlung. [K. 177; His 294 and 299]

A sense of primeval purpose, latent power and confidence in victory is expressed in this cycle: "The Sixteen Standard-bearers of the Confederate States". It is from sword and banner, the symbols of battle and victory, that these pictures derive both unity and variety. Figure and banner dominate the picture-space and seem almost to burst its bounds. The primitive violence of stride and stance characteristic of the whole series is accentuated by the white-on-black effect.

The invention of this white-on-black technique is attributed to Graf.

125
The Satyr's Family

White-on-black woodcut. Monotype. 8 × 4 5/8 in. Dated 1520. Signed: Dagger monogram on a tablet. Basle: Öffentliche Kunstsammlung. [His 283; K. 174]

Dürer's engraving of 1505 with its idyllic representation of the *Satyr and his Family* (B. 69) gave Graf the idea for this woodcut. It is not a borrowed composition, however, but an original version of the subject to which Graf's white-on-black method imparted the precision of a drawing.

This new technique retained the original sharpness of the drawing far better than the ordinary woodcut, as the carver had only to follow the lines Graf had drawn upon the block. Whereas Dürer's engraving is three-dimensional in composition, Graf's design has the character of a surface decoration of which the elements stand out in attractive relief.

126

Page of Calligraphy (in cipher)

Pen drawing. 12^1/$_4$×7^1/$_8$ in. Dated 1523. (Reverse of the pen drawing reproduced as Plate 18). Basle: Öffentliche Kunstsammlung. [K. 111a]

Graf's cipher, also used in the etching reproduced as Plate 121, belongs to the elementary type (known as the Caesarian System) in which each letter is replaced by a number, a sign or another letter. The text, deciphered by Dr. Eduard His-Heusler, is a German translation of an ancient antiphon to the Holy Ghost still used in the Roman Catholic liturgy: *Veni Sancte Spiritus, reple tuorum corda fidelium et tui amoris in eis ignem accende, qui per diversitatem linguarum cunctas gentes in unitate fidei congregasti* (for this text we are indebted to Rev. F. Blum of Basle). A slightly different German version of the antiphon appeared in Luther's hymn-book *Enchiridion* published in Erfurt in 1527 (Major).

To Graf's translation is appended the enciphered signature: "By me, Ursus Graf, goldsmith and die-cutter to the mint in Basle, anno 1523".

The initial capital represents a skull in a charnel house and bears the same date.

127

Venal Love

Woodcut. Monotype. 12^3/$_4$×8^3/$_4$ in. 1511 (Parker). Signed: V G monogram (centre) and borax box (extreme right). London: British Museum. [K. 180]

This fine woodcut was discovered twenty years ago by Parker (*Anzeiger für Schweizerische Altertumskunde*, 1922, p. 93 et seq.). Like so many of these broadsheet woodcuts which were nailed up on the walls of rooms it is now known only from this one print, the sole survivor of what was probably a large and popular edition. As late as 1565, the composition reappears in a rather free adaptation as the subject of a tapestry which passed from the collections of Meyer-am Rhyn and Roman Abt of Lucerne to the Figdor Collection in Vienna. (Major, p. 236/7.— B. Kurth, *Die deutschen Bildteppiche des Mittelalters*, Vienna 1926, I, p. 121).

The theme was a commonplace of the time, but a new zest is lent to the satire by the popular idiom in which it is presented. It was just the kind of picture that appealed to the common man, who, after feasting his eyes upon its images of earthly pleasure, must have dwelt with gloomy gusto upon the crude rhyming "*memento mori*" which may be translated "Death

endeth all, heed thou my warning, All earthly joy doth end in mourning".

Parker has suggested that the signature may be a forgery and the work a pastiche. This possibility cannot be entirely set aside. The figures of the young woman and her wooers are not characteristic, nor do we know any other composition in which Graf combines three figures in so lucid a manner. He had on the other hand often made equally original and decorative use of the scroll.

128

Eight Men in Conversation

Woodcut. Early monotype. 12^1/$_2$×8^3/$_4$ in. Circa 1506/07 (Koegler). Signed: VG monogram. Basle: Öffentliche Kunstsammlung. [His 275; K. 158; Koegler, Beiträge No. H. 277]

This print owes its clarity to the skill of an expert blockcutter. The design itself is a clever combination of variously derived material. Although the origin of the unusual heads and poses remains uncertain, the man on the extreme left recalls Dürer's engraving of *The Prodigal Son* (B. 28). The origin of the background is equally uncertain although the motif often recurs in woodcut illustrations. The man with his back turned and a cloak hung loosely over his shoulders is the only traceable borrowing. He is a copy of the figure of Ascanius from a woodcut, the *Duel of Dares and Entelius*, in a Virgil published by Johann Grüninger in Strasbourg in 1502. Graf has merely replaced the scroll above the original head by an elegantly curled ostrich feather. (Cf. Major, p. 150, note 22.) Besides this direct borrowing, Graf's early woodcuts contain stylistic evidence of relationship with the work of the Strasbourg masters. This is one of Graf's best woodcuts.

129

Pyramus and Thisbe

Woodcut. Early monotype. 12^3/$_8$×8^3/$_4$ in. Circa 1506/07 (Koegler). Signed: VG monogram. Basle: Öffentliche Kunstsammlung. [His 277; Koegler, Beiträge No. H. 277]

But for the monogram we should not have known this to be a work of Graf. The fact that he drew the same subject in a much livelier manner (Plate 71), although almost twenty years later and admittedly in a farcial mood, would have made the ascription even more unlikely. It shows all the defects of a youthful work. His most unhappy Pyramus and the figure of Thisbe wringing her hands are obviously copied, and the landscape with its neatly conventional trees, mountains and clouds gives no inkling of Graf's later style. It is moreover strongly reminiscent of Dürer's early woodcuts, such as the *Martyrdom of St. Catherine* (B. 120). We can picture the young apprentice vainly endeavouring to reconcile the details of his borrowed material. The quest for perspective is expressed by the winding path; the reflection of the moon in the water-trough is an unsuccessful attempt to light the scene; the Hebraic tombstone is supposed to indicate the antiquity and foreign origin of the Babylonian legend. The whole work reveals awkwardness and perplexity. Only in the attitude of the peasant squatting on the fountain can we find any hint of character as expressed in Graf's later figures.

130
Christ before Caiphas

Woodcut. 8 1/2 × 6 1/8 in. 1503. First printed in Ringmann's "Passion", Strasbourg, Joh. Knobloch, 1506. Signed: Separated initials V G. [His 12; K. 156]

Ringmann's „Passion" was published by Johann Knobloch of Strasbourg in 1506. It contained a series of twenty-five woodcuts which had been designed by Graf as early as 1503. These were Graf's first woodcuts and Strasbourg the starting-point of his fame. These first attempts have the uncouth vigour of primitive popular art. It would be pointless to trace the varied influences which formed them, for Graf did not hesitate to copy anything that suited his purpose. He masked defects of composition by a resourceful disposition of side-scenes and props and of white or hatched planes, devices which bear witness to his instinctive recognition of the integrating power of the straight line. In his later drawings, the straight lines of dagger, pike and sword determine the composition.

131
Christ and the Holy Virgin interceding for a supplicant Sinner

Woodcut. Monotype. 5 7/8 × 4 3/4 in. Dated 1514. Signed: V G monogram and Basle staff. Basle: Öffentliche Kunstsammlung. [His 279; K. 167]

At the fairs held in front of churches and monasteries, this type of religious picture had a large sale. It gave the pious man visible assurance of the efficacy of his prayer, and its price was a tangible offering which could not fail to procure him a hearing in heaven.

Graf designed this devotional picture with the utmost care. The Virgin's outstretched forefinger reveals the importance he attached to the formal relation of the figures. He succeeded in the difficult task of fulfilling popular pictorial demands with formal artistic effect.

132
The Pope Title-Page

Woodcut. 9 1/4 × 7 5/8 in. Signed: V G monogram and VRSVS on left border. Used by the Amerbach, Petri and Froben printing houses, Basle 1511. [His 281]

The Pope is giving audience to a delegation of lawyers and monks who present him with a volume of Decretals. The five roundels represent the five subdivisions of the Decretals: "*Judex, Judicium, Clerus, Sponsalia, Crimen*". We can distinguish with certainty between the original and the borrowed features of the design, since it was based on the woodcut title-page of a book published in Paris in 1510. Graf's chief contribution is the row of cherubs romping along the arch. The chief merit of the picture lies in its three-dimensional composition. It owes much of its effect to the low eye-level to which Graf was particularly addicted, to the unusually close co-ordination of the figures, to the use of cast shadows, and to the receding curve of the canopy. This woodcut is not therefore a mere copy of its predecessor; although still mediaeval in concept, it is an original artistic creation.

133
Humanitas Title-page

Woodcut. 10 3/4 × 6 7/8 in. Printed in several books published by Johann Froben, Basle, 1513. Signed V G monogram on a tablet. [His 314]

This title-page was used by Froben for various books printed in and after 1513. Graf borrowed the architectural framework from an Italian design (Ferrara, 1497) and considerably enhanced its effect by the use of relief. Although the scholar Beatus Rhenanus, who had settled in Basle in 1511 and become reader to the printing house, probably advised him upon the treatment of this page, Graf was not discouraged from using his imagination.

He interpreted the allegory with delightful ingenuousness: *Humanitas*, in a tiny triumphal car flanked by *putti* bearing heraldic shields, is being pushed or hauled along by Virgil, Homer, Cicero and Demosthenes. Standing upon columns beneath baldaquins on either side of the title are the figures of Kairos, god of opportunity, and Nemesis, goddess of avenging justice. The festoons, cornucopias and angel-heads are derived from the Italian design. In this design Graf gave relief to every detail with painstaking thoroughness. Once more we note his preoccupation with cast shadow, here used to give its effect of solidity to the epitaph-shaped frame.

Copies of the design by later artists pay implicit tribute to its merit.

134
Emperor Maximilian Title-Page

Woodcut. 11 7/8 × 8 3/8 in. *Divini Gregorii Nyssae Episcopi libri octo*, Strasbourg, Matthias Schürer, May 1512. Signed: V G monogram on a shield. [His 313]

The title-page is a work of homage to the Emperor Maximilian, a ruler highly esteemed by the Humanists. Graf is scarcely to blame for the mediocrity of its design, for he was obliged to include every detail calculated to enrich Beatus Rhenanus' intended compliment, and, first and foremost, the escutcheons of the twenty hereditary fiefs and those of the seven electors which surround the imperial arms. On the left and right of the Emperor stand his grandsons and successors, Charles and Ferdinand. In the upper left-hand corner is the portrait of a papal legate in the form of an antique cameo. Greek quotations are strewn here and there to glorify the imperial rule. Of the four inscribed tablets, two, bearing the titles of Charles and Ferdinand, are set obliquely, thus fulfilling the same function as those in Holbein's Amerbach portrait of 1519. At the foot of the page, on an antique votive tablet, is inscribed in lapidary characters the dedication to the Emperor composed by Beatus Rhenanus.

Little space remained for the expression of Graf's own ideas. The ornamental borders are carefully but lifelessly drawn. Only in the figures of the trophy-supporters and of the elfish *putti* did his originality reveal itself. In the attitude of the man leaning on his staff, and in the disposition of the hands of his companion, we can already recognise characteristics of Graf's later figures. This title-page shows that Graf fully appreciated the value in page-decoration of his special talent for detailed surface relief.

135–138, 144–145
Six Woodcuts from two Tales of Chivalry

Hystorie von Olwier und Artus and *Hystorie von Valentin und Orsus*, translated into German by Wilhelm Ziely, Basle, Adam Petri, February 1521. Unsigned.

135
Lady on Horseback and Cavalcade

2 3/4 × 5 3/8 in. [Koegler, Beiträge No. 367, 1]

136
Soldiers aboard a Sailing Ship

2 3/4 × 5 3/8 in. [l. c. No. 367, 3]

137
A Tournament

2 3/4 × 5 1/4 in. [l. c. No. 367, 2]

138
A pitched Battle

2 3/4 × 5 1/4 in. [l. c. No. 367, 4]

144
Lovers in a Turret

2 3/4 × 2 5/8 in. [l. c. No. 368, 5]

145
Couple dancing to Drum and Fife

2 3/4 × 2 5/8 in. [l. c. No. 368, 14]

These woodcuts for the two Tales of Chivalry rank among Graf's best and most original illustrations. Their success was due partly to the fact that he was able to rely almost entirely upon his own imagination, but above all to his gift for simple and vivid pictorial narrative. The fresh gaiety and zest with which these little scenes are presented reveal Graf's sure instinct for pictorial effect.

There is no sign of the apprentice in these works; an occasional clumsiness of detail is probably due to the deficiencies of the block-cutter. Several of the poses already developed by Graf in his drawings are put to account and skilfully adapted to the requirements of the composition. (Cf. Plate 47 for the Battle, and Plate 87 for the Drum and Fife.) The comparatively small size of the woodcuts seems to have favoured the solution of more complicated composition problems than Graf generally attacked in his drawings.

139
A Classroom

Woodcut. 4 3/8 × 3 1/4 in. Dr. Kungsperger's Almanac, Zurich, Hans am Wasen, 1508. Unsigned. [His 33]

The Virgin is presenting the Christ Child to the schoolmaster who is giving a lesson to two other boys. The *stanza* supplies the dialogue appropriate to the scene. The atmosphere of the workshop appears to have deprived Graf of his natural zest for narrative; this woodcut is well drawn but unambitious and shows little sign of originality.

140
The Escutcheons of the Sixteen States of the Confederation and the Imperial Arms

Woodcuts. 6 3/8 × 4 1/8 in. Henricus Glareanus, *Panegyricus in laudatissimum Helvetiorum foedus*, Basle, Adam Petri, 1515. Signed: V G monogram on a tablet. [His 301; Koegler, Beiträge No. H. 301]

The imperial poet laureate Henricus Glareanus related the history of the Confederation in noble hexameters imbued with humanistic scholarship. Adam Petri published this panegyric with a title-page designed by Graf. Small woodcuts of the shields and supporters of the thirteen states and of the three allied states of St. Gall, Valais and Coire were combined to form a single block surmounted by the imperial arms. The unity of the sixteen states, extolled with pious zeal by the learned Glareanus in the course of a lengthy poem, was thus expressed by Graf in simultaneous picture. The lively contrast of the supporters' attitudes expresses the idea of variety in unity. These little coats of arms reveal Graf's talent for heraldic design and his ability to use a narrow field to the best advantage.

141
Sermon and Confession

Woodcut. 3 1/2 × 4 3/4 in. Used in conjunction with an ornamental woodcut for the title-page of Michael Lochmayer, *Parochiale Curatorum*, Basle, Michael Furter, 1514. Unsigned. [Koegler, Beiträge No. 345]

In this unpretentious little picture Graf related the two groups which enact "sermon" and "confession" in a well-ordered spatial composition. Essentials of pose are skilfully expressed; the two women in the foreground are excellently observed. The half-turned back of the seated woman is particularly interesting.

142
The Lute-player

Woodcut. 3 1/2 × 2 5/8 in. Sebastian Virdung, *Musica getutscht*, Basle, Michael Furter, 1511. Signed: V G monogram. [His 303]

In this charming woodcut illustrating a guide to lute-playing, the block-cutter followed the original design with unusual care and retained much of the spontaneity of the drawn line. Graf used the same pose two years later for an engraving of a seated soldier of approximately the same size as this woodcut (Cf. Plate 120).

143, 146–148 *
Book Ornaments
143
Capital A with a Cherub

Woodcut 1 3/8 × 1 3/8 in. From an alphabet used by Adam Petri, Basle, from 1516. Unsigned. [Major, p. 140; Koegler, Beiträge No. 406]

---

* For Nos. 144 and 145 see left column.

146
Gothic foliated Scroll with Pomegranate

Woodcut border. 5/8 × 5 3/4 in. *Opuscula Plutarchi*, Basle, Johann Froben, 1514. Unsigned. [Koegler, Beiträge No. 387]

147
Scroll

Woodcut border. 5/8 × 5 3/4 in. Erasmus, *Adagia*, Basle, Johann Froben, 1513. Unsigned. [His 327, d]

148
Bagpipes, Dice, Basle Shield, Jester's Cap, and Lute

Woodcut border 5/8 × 5 3/4 in. Philipp Engelbrecht, *Friburgica*, Basle, Johann Froben, 1515. Unsigned. (The lute appears in the same form on the knife-sheath, Plate 98). [Koegler, Beiträge No. 386]

Graf had an inexhaustible fund of ideas for initials, borders and every kind of book ornament. These four examples show the variety of his designs. His skill is revealed above all in his use of simple and foliated scrolls. The simple spiral development of his foliated scroll is a basic element of Graf's ornament. Even when he employed Renaissance forms, his Gothic style triumphed in the development of the design; it was by this Gothic use of relief that he achieved his most lively effects.

149
Headpiece of a Wall-Almanac

3 woodcuts. Almanac published by Pamphilus Gengenbach, Basle, 1519. Used from 1513. Unsigned. Basle: Öffentliche Kunstsammlung. [K. 164]

Saint Damian
4 1/8 × 3 1/2 in. [Koegler, Beiträge No. 341]

Saint Cosmas
4 1/8 × 3 1/2 in. [l. c. No. 342]

Sectioned Human Figure and Signs of the Zodiac
4 1/8 × 3 3/4 in. [l. c. No. 343]

The pious legend of the brothers Cosmas and Damian relates how their selfless devotion to the cure of the sick converted multitudes to the Christian faith. They were venerated in the Middle Ages as the patron saints of doctors and apothecaries. Their attributes are the urine flask, ointment box and spatula. Together with the anatomical subject, their figures were a suitable decoration for an almanac which provided its purchaser with a rich gallimaufry of medical advice, religious instruction and astrological lore.

We reproduce on a smaller scale part of a large page printed in red and black from an almanac for the year 1519. Graf must have designed the woodcuts some time before, as they had already appeared in an almanac for 1513. The terse vigour of the little pictures must have made them popular, for the blocks were used over a long period.

150
Virgin and Child
The Emperor Henry II and Saint Pantalus

Woodcut. 4 1/4 × 7 3/8 in. Dated 1514. Signed: V G monogram. Title-page of *Breviarium Basiliense*, Basle, Jacob von Pforzheim, 1515. [His 271; K. 168]

In the centre stands the Virgin with the Child in her arms, her figure enveloped in the mandorla. On her right is the Emperor Henry II who completed the building of Basle Cathedral; on her left stands Saint Pantalus, legendary first bishop of Basle. At the feet of these three patrons of the city are ranged the shield of Bishop Christoph von Utenheim (1502–1527), the imperial arms and the arms of Basle. The crescent moon upon which the Virgin traditionally stood is transformed into an arched pedestal, which also serves as frame to the episcopal arms. Developing this semi-architectural idea, Graf made the arch spring from a horizontal line which cuts off the picture just below the ankles of the figures.

151
Two Soldiers and a Woman watched by Death

Woodcut. Monotype. 8 × 4 5/8 in. Dated 1524. Signed: Dagger monogram. Basle: Öffentliche Kunstsammlung. [His 280; K. 178]

This picture was conceived in those deep recesses of the mind where individual experience becomes one with that of all humanity. Its theme was carried beyond mere personal interpretation and endowed with the universal meaning of a parable. Hence the unusual power—one might almost say grandeur—of its impression. For it is an impression and no longer a message; here Graf illustrates no story, points no moral, voices no social comment. He merely gives co-existence to four figures and leaves each one to tell his own story. The two warriors personify the ancient fighting spirit of the Swiss, founded in steadfastness and self-reliance. By their side sits Vice who has assumed female form and is the secret ally of Death. The transience of all human actions, desires and aspirations is symbolised by the figure of Death sitting upon the naked branch of the tree and holding out his hour-glass upon which a raven is perched.

This woodcut is one of Graf's finest achievements. Its details may have derived from Wächtlin, Cranach or Holbein, but Graf transformed them into essential parts of an original whole. An expert block-cutter (Koegler suggests it may have been Lützelburger) gave to the print all the fine qualities of the drawing.

As if to demonstrate the power concentrated in each figure, Willem Liefrink of Antwerp carved a replica of the picture from which he omitted the upper half with the lurking figure of Death. Even when shorn of this important figure, the picture retains its effect.

Erwin Gradmann

Bibliography

His, Eduard. *Urs Graf, Goldschmied, Münzstempelgraveur und Formschneider*. Zahn's Jahrbücher für Kunstwissenschaft VI, 1873, p.145ff. . . . . . . Quoted as: His.

Koegler, Hans. *Beiträge zum Holzschnittwerk des Urs Graf*. Anzeiger für Schweizerische Altertumskunde 1907, p.43, 132, 213ff. . . . . . Quoted as: Koegler, Beiträge

Koegler, Hans. *Beschreibendes Verzeichnis der Basler Handzeichnungen des Urs Graf*. Basel 1926 . . . . Quoted as: K.

Lüthi, Walter. *Urs Graf und die Kunst der alten Schweizer*. Zürich 1928.

Major, Emil. *Urs Graf, ein Beitrag zur Geschichte der Goldschmiedekunst im 16. Jahrhundert*. Strassburg 1907. Mit Biographie und urkundlichen Texten. . . Quoted as: Major.

Major, Emil. *Die Bildnisse Urs Grafs und seiner Gattin*. Basler Zeitschrift für Geschichte und Altertumskunde VI, 1907, p.152ff.

Parker, Karl Th. *Die verstreuten Handzeichnungen Urs Grafs*. Anzeiger für schweizerische Altertumskunde 1921, p.207ff. . . . . Quoted as: P.

Parker, Karl Th. *Zwanzig Federzeichnungen von Urs Graf*. Zürich 1922.

Reproductions

I

2

3

4

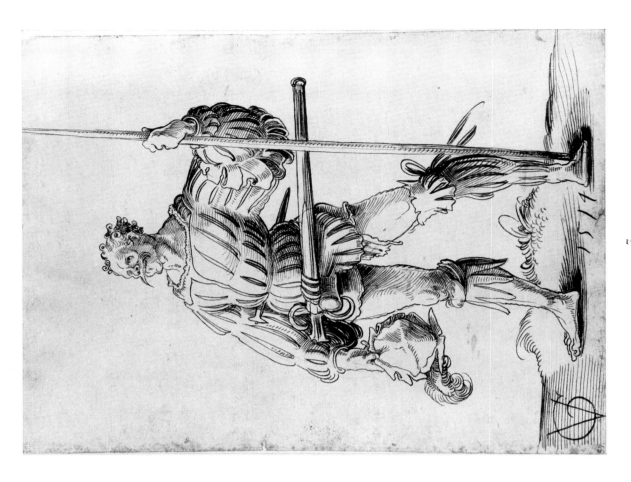

7

6

6

8

II

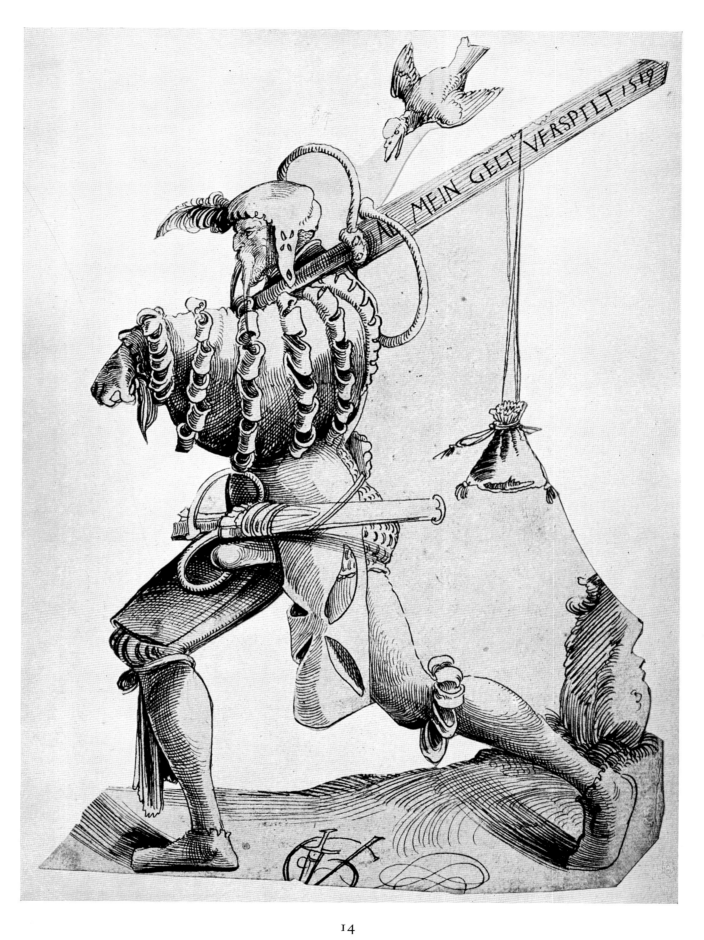

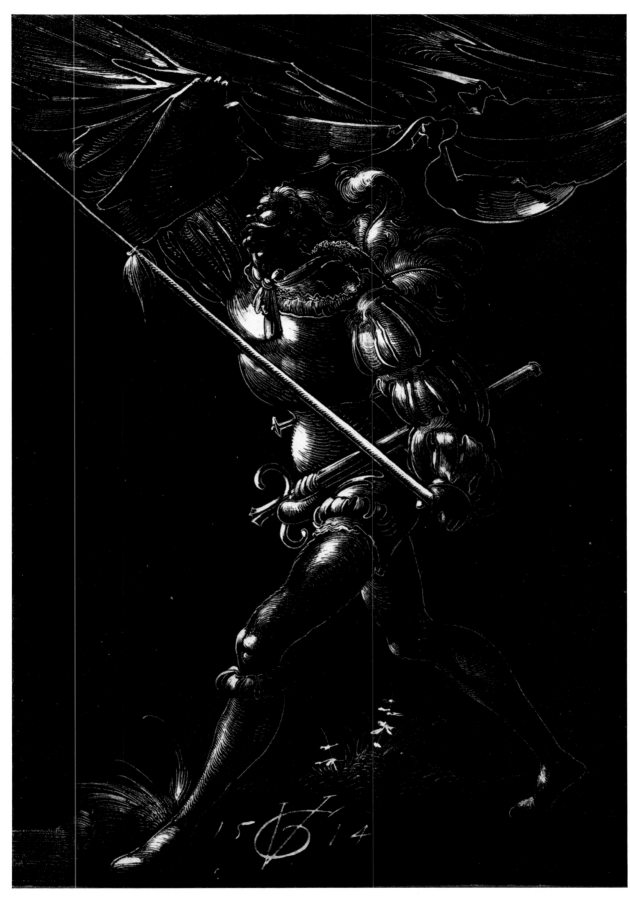

16

18

19

20

NELI ICH WOT GERN

22

23

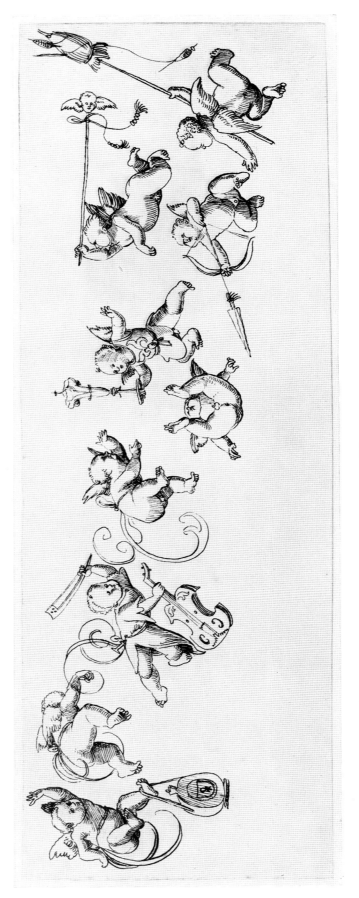

24

25

M. S. R. M.

28

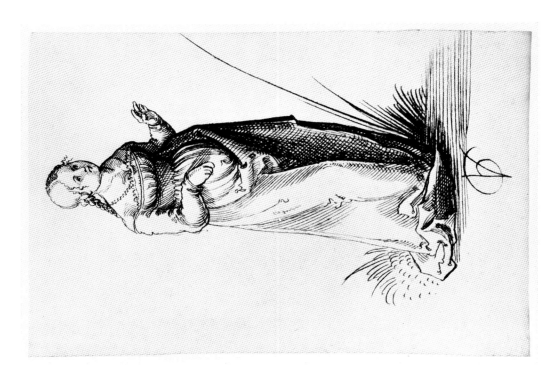

27

29

31

15 ✶ 16

32

33

34

35

37

36

GOT·GEB·VSGLVK

GLVK·VF·MINER·STEN

38

40

41

42

43

1 5 1 5

44

45

48

49

50

53

57

61

64

65

66

RETIBVI · HCI · REFPO · RID ·
SAD · VD · SAD · ILBIW · TSESOL · RIM

1513

ARISTOTLES

1 5 1 4

72

73

74

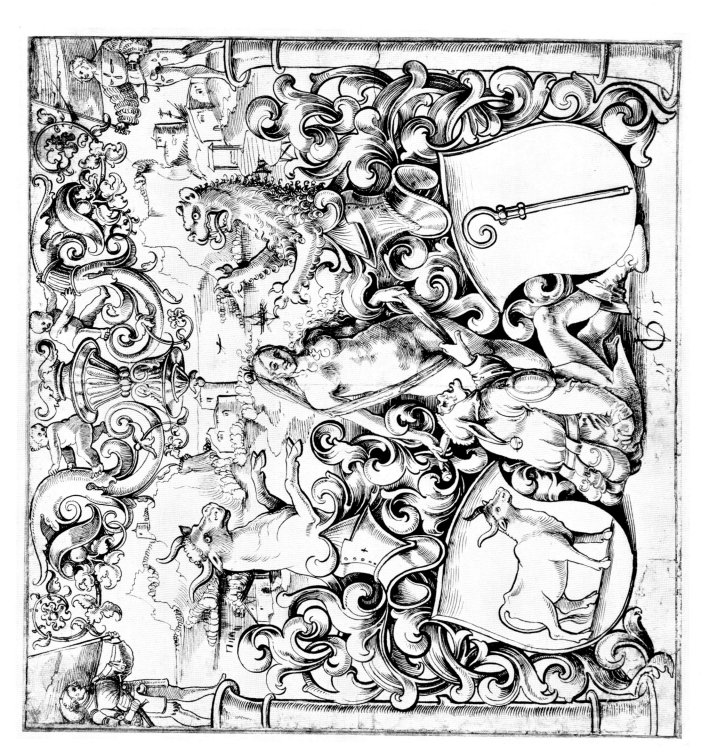

1521

80

81

82

84

86

87

88

89

91

90

92

93

94

96

95

97

98   99

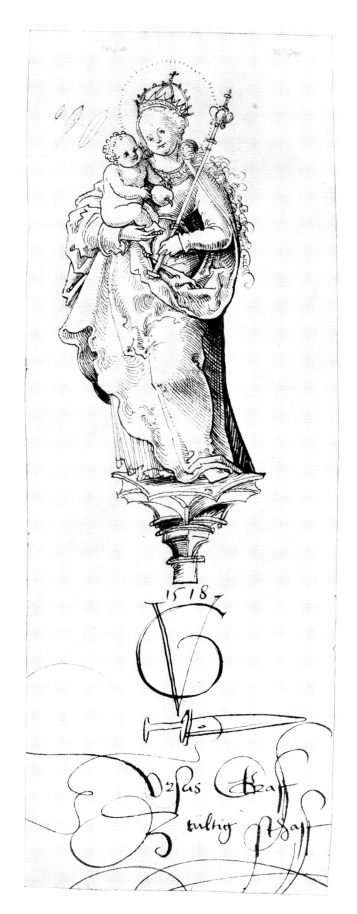

100

101

102

105

103

104

106

107

108

109

110

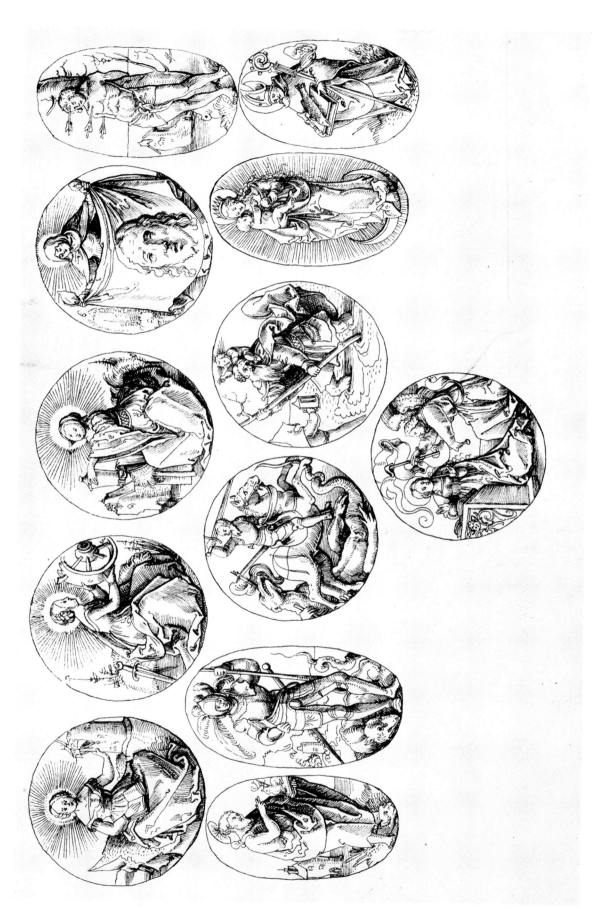

III

112

114

115

113

116

119

117

118

122

121

120

LVZER

WALLIS ·

125

das ist mein rot. Wañ alle ding beschlüst das end Bedēʒ der todt,

·PVRAMVS·

Sic scdos ponu

Blasphemauit,

131

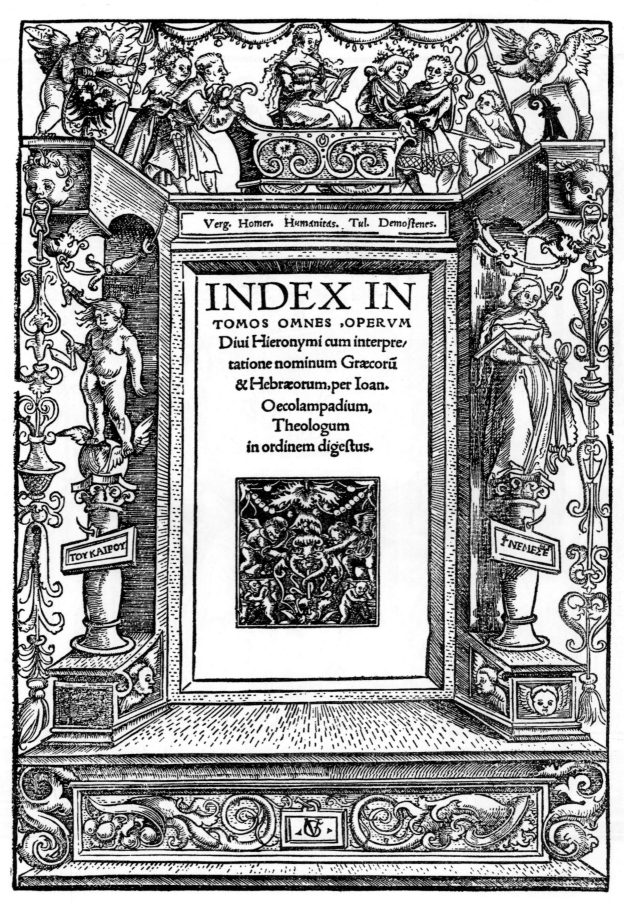

Verg. Homer. Humanitas. Tul. Demoſtenes.

INDEX IN
TOMOS OMNES ,OPERVM
Diui Hieronymi cum interpre=
tatione nominum Græcorū
& Hebræorum, per Ioan.
Oecolampadium,
Theologum
in ordinem digeſtus.

133

EIΣ ΚΟΙΡΑΝΟΣ ΕΣΤΩ ΕΙΣ ΒΑΣΙΛΕΥΣ ΒΟΥΛΗΦΟΡΟΣ ΑΝΑΞ
ᾼ ΛΑΟΙ ΤΕ ΓΙ ΤΕΤΡΑΦΕΤΑΙ ΚΑΙ ΤΟΣΣΑ ΜΕΜΗΛΕ

CAROL·FLANDR·
COMES·ARCHID·
AVSTR·DVX·BVR·
GVND

FERDINAND·REX·C
STELLÆ·ET·LEGIO
NIS·ARCHIDVX·
AVSTRIÆ

MAXIMI+LIANVS·AVG·

DIVINI
Gregorij Nyssæ Episcopi qui fuit frater
Basilij Magni LIBRI OCTO.
I   De Homine.
II   De Anima.
III De Elementis.
IIII De Viribus animæ.
V   De volūtario et inuolūtario
VI   De Fato.
VII De Libero arbitrio.
VIII De Prouidentia.

IMPER·CÆS·MAXIMILIANO·
P·F·AVG·PATRI·PATRIÆ·LIBER
TATISQVE·ADSERTORI·BEAT·
RHENANVS·   F·C·

ΟΥΚ ΑΓΑΘ ΟΝ ΠΟΛΥΚΟΙΡΑΝΙΗ ΕΙΣ ΚΟΙΡΑΝΟΣ ΕΣΤΩ

135

136

137

138

Ich han min kind erzogen zart vnd schon
Vnd wolt es gern zů schůl lassen gon
Vnd bit üch durch got vnd ere
Das ir min kind trülich wöllent lere
Liebe frow ich wil es gern leren
Vnd min bestes zů im keren

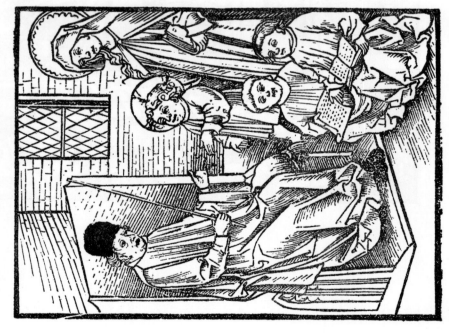

141

142

143

144

145

146

147

148